IN QUEST
OF THE
HOLY GRAAL

IN QUEST
OF THE
HOLY GRAAL

SEBASTIAN EVANS, LL.D.

Athens ‡ Manchester

In Quest of the Holy Graal

Published by: Old Book Publishing Ltd

Book Cover Design: Old Book Publishing Ltd

Title of original: In Quest of the Holy Graal

Originally published in 1898 by J. M. Dent & CO in London

Cover Image: The Damsel of the Sanct Grael by *Dante Gabriel Rossetti*

ISBN–10: 1-78107-170-5
ISBN–13: 978-1-78107-170-0

EDITOR'S NOTE

IN QUEST OF
THE HOLY GRAAL

AN INTRODUCTION TO THE
STUDY OF THE LEGEND BY
SEBASTIAN EVANS, LL.D.

SHADOWS WE ARE &
DEPARTING WE FADE

LONDON
J. M. DENT AND CO.
ALDINE HOUSE
1898

TO MY FELLOW - WORKERS,

ENGLISH AND FOREIGN, IN

THE FIELD OF THE GRAAL

CONTENTS

I

PERCEVAL

Vergente mundi vespere
Novum sidus exoritur
Et clausis culpe carcere
Preco Salutis mittitur.

Doctrinam evangelicam
Spargens per orbis cardinem
Pestem fugat hereticam
Novum producens Ordinem.

In festo B. Dominici.

A MYSTERY from the first has enshrouded the
Legend of the Graal. That the Graal was
intended in some way to typify the Sacrament
of the Holy Communion is abundantly clear
from a thousand passages in the various versions
of the story. All beyond this primary indica-
tion is indefinite, shadowy, impalpable. Yet
we feel as we read that the words employed are
intended to convey some deeper meaning than
the fiction bears on the face of it. The romance
is more than a romance. It is also a secret

A

written in cipher. Its mysticism is as marked
as its mystery. Throughout, there is a con-
tinual suggestion of hidden meanings, a re-
current insistence on things seen as types and
symbols of things unseen. When Malory tells
us that ' thistory of the Sancgreal is cronycled for
one of the truest and the holiest that is in thys
world,' or an earlier poet that it was written by
the hand of Our Lord Himself, it is clear that
they meant to draw a clear line of demarcation
between this story and the older secular romances
of Arthur and his knights. But wherein lies
the difference between them? What is the
key of the cipher? What is the Presence
that haunts and hints at every turn in the path
that lies through the hallowed ground?

Take the groundwork of the story told in
the 'High History of the Holy Graal.'

Every incident recorded bears more or less
directly on the history of Yglais, the widowed
Lady of the Valleys of Camelot, and her three
royal brethren—King Fisherman, King Pelles
' of the Lower Folk,' and the King of Castle
Mortal. These trace their unrecorded ancestry
up to Joseph of Abarimacie, the good soldier of
Pilate who took down the body of the Saviour
from hanging on the cross. The husband of
Yglais was Alain li Gros, the eldest of twelve

knights, all of whom died in arms within twelve years of being made knight. They were lineal descendants of 'Nichodemus.' Alain li Gros and Yglais had one daughter, Dindrane, and one son, Perceval, the hero of the romance.

The theme of the epos is an error rather than a sin of omission. The Rich King Fisherman dwells in the Castle of the Graal, where the most holy Vessel is enshrined in a most holy chapel. On a time, his nephew, Perceval, visits the Rich King at his castle. The King, his household, and his guests are served from the Graal itself by a damsel with golden hair. Blood from the point of a lance falls mystically into the holy Vessel drop by drop, but the food distributed is abundant for all, and the savour is sweeter than that of any earthly meat. Perceval partakes with the rest ; but although he beholds the Graal three several times, forbears or forgets to ask what the wondrous food may be, and who may be those to whom it is distributed. This failure to ask the fateful question is the well-spring of sorrow and manifold tribulation. 'Of one little word that he delayed to speak came to pass so sore mischance in Greater Britain that all the lands and all the islands fell thereby into much sorrow.' 'All lands were commoved to war thereby, nor never thereafter might knight meet other but he should fight with him in arms upon none other occasion.' The Damsel with golden hair becomes suddenly bald, and the Rich King Fisherman falls into a grievous 'languishment' of which he can never be healed save by another good knight appearing at his Castle and asking the question which Perceval left unasked. Gawain arrives, and the Graal twice appears before him, but no word of inquiry passes his lips. Lancelot arrives, but not even a sight of the Graal is vouchsafed to him on account of his love for Guenievre, Arthur's Queen. Before any knight has arrived to break the spell, King Fisherman dies, and his wicked brother, the King of Castle Mortal, usurps the Castle of the Graal. Perceval besieges the castle, which he enters in triumph just as his unrighteous uncle in despair stabs himself to the heart on the topmost wall, and drops headlong into the river beneath, which is the River of Hell. Perceval now enjoys his rightful heritage in peace and honour. The Graal, which has disappeared while the King of Castle Mortal usurps the Castle of the Graal, presents itself again in the most holy chapel, together with the mystic lance, 'for our Lord God loved the place much.' It has three names—'Eden,' 'Castle of Joy,' and 'Castle of Souls.'

This is the pivot of the story. The various episodes incidentally connected with the main story and the continuation of the story itself I do not here propose to discuss. If the central conception of the romance is once clearly understood, the rest will fall naturally into place and suggest its own interpretation. My principal object is to identify Perceval himself and the group of personages directly associated with him, more particularly King Fisherman and Gawain; to determine the nature and significance of the question which Perceval neglected to ask at the Castle of the Graal; to ascertain what were the 'mischances that fell on Greater Britain,' and to show in what way they were the result of Perceval's neglect. If these cardinal identifications are established, the general drift of the legend will be sufficiently clear to indicate its relations to the older legends of Arthur, with which I have nothing here to do. The towers of Camelot and Joyous-Gard, the laundes and forests of Lyonesse and Broceliand, lie beyond the limits of my quest. Such adventures as are here met with befall only either in or between the realm of Logres and the Castle of the Graal.

Who, then, is Perceval, the hero of the story? He is one of Arthur's knights, but his relations with Arthur are of a wholly different order from those of any other knight. Never once, from first to last, does Perceval take his seat at the Table Round among the other knights of Arthur. Arthur comes to Perceval's Castle of the Graal, but it is as seeker and learner. He is but a humble follower in the footsteps of Perceval. If Arthur and Gawain can be said to achieve the Quest of the Graal at all, it is only by finding it in Perceval's most holy chapel. The story only implies, it does not explicitly tell us, that the Graal appeared to them. Earthly knight and king are never once admitted to the higher level of the spiritual knighthood of Perceval. Lancelot himself never so much as sees the Graal. The story throughout is the apotheosis of spiritual as distinguished from temporal chivalry.

So much, indeed, is common to all versions of the legend. The superiority of spiritual to temporal knighthood is insisted on as strongly by Malory as by the writer of the High History. But, read in this light, surely the pedigree of Perceval here given offers no impenetrable mystery? His mother is Yglais. Whose son was the hero of a spiritual romance likely to be, if not of holy Mother Church ? The very word itself is simply one mediæval way of spelling the modern French *église*. Here, at least, the author has no desire to conceal his meaning. Who Perceval himself may be, he leaves to be inferred from his history, but he will leave no room for doubt that he is a son of Mother Church. Nor, at the time the romance was written, was the name of Perceval's father less easy to understand. Alain li Gros is, in fact, historically and accurately represented as the spiritual father of Perceval. Alan the Great, Alanus de Insulis, Alain de l'Isle, is none other than the once famous *Doctor Universalis*, whose history may be read at large in the sixteenth volume of the *Histoire Littéraire de la France*. Here it is sufficient to note that about 1174 he became a monk at Canterbury, and accompanied the Archbishop to the memorable Lateran Council of 1179. While at Rome on this occasion, he was commissioned by Alexander III. to write against the Albigenses and other heretics, a task to which he brought a keenness of intellect and a knowledge of Latinity only equalled by the fervour of his orthodoxy. In the year of his return from Rome, he was made Prior of Christchurch at Canterbury; and in 1186, Abbot of Tewkesbury,

where he wrote his life of S. Thomas of Canterbury. Finally, he retired to the Abbey of
Cîteaux, where he died apparently in the year
1201. The dates are noteworthy. The
romance was obviously written after Alain's
death, but at a time when his name and fame
were still in all men's mouths. More noteworthy still is the fact that the work of
Perceval's father Alain against the Albigenses
formed no small portion of the spiritual
armoury of the preachers who wrought and
fought in the Albigensian crusade; itself, as
will be seen presently, an event closely connected with the 'High History' of the Holy
Graal.

The identification of two other members of
Perceval's family is not less easy and certain.
The Rich King Fisherman is as obviously the
Pope as Yglais is obviously the Church. There
is only one potentate who bears the title. To-
day, as when the story was written, the Pope
at times wears the 'Fisherman's ring,' and
now, as then, makes use of it to seal a certain
portion of his private correspondence. The
Romancer could not have hit on a happier
title for the Sovereign Pontiff who occupies
the throne founded by the fisherman of Galilee.
The King of Castle Mortal wears a disguise

equally slight. His features are as clearly drawn and as clearly recognisable. There is 'as much bad in him as there is good in his two brethren.' His throne is in the Castle of Mortality, not in the Castle of the Graal. He is the Chief of the temporal world, as his brother is Chief of the spiritual world. If the Rich King Fisherman is the Pope, the King of Castle Mortal can be none other than the Emperor. The first draught of the romance may possibly have been sketched out in the reign of the fourth Otho. It was certainly finished in that of the second Frederic. Either one or the other may well have been the original of the unfavourable portrait drawn by the orthodox romancer.

The third brother is less easy to identify, because his real history is less familiar than that of Pope or Emperor. The time, moreover, during which even a romancer would be justified in describing him as king at all was very limited. Twenty years before the book was written, it might have been barely possible to regard him as King of the Lesser Folk—*li rois de basse gent*. Twenty years after, it would have been impossible. In his royal capacity he belongs to the age of the romance and to no other. Once identified, however, the identi-

fication is as certain as that of the others. No
alternative suggestion is possible. He is the
Abbot of Cîteaux.

The extraordinary predominance of the
Cistercian Order in the early years of the
thirteenth century is one of the marvels of
history. From the days of Bernard of Clairvaux, the re-founder of the Order, if the Pope
was the head of the Church Militant, the Abbots
of Cîteaux had been as generally recognised
as the heads of what may be termed the Church
Military. All the great semi-monastic Orders
of Knighthood, the Templars, the Hospitallers,
and many others, were more or less closely
affiliated to Cîteaux. When a crusade was
declared, the necessary arrangements, the
preaching, the organisation, the general jurisdiction—in the case of the Albigensian Crusade,
even the military command—were all delegated
to the Abbot of Cîteaux. The Cistercian
Order, in fact, was the executive of the Papacy
in its temporal aspect. The relations between
Pope and Abbot are repeatedly referred to in
the letters of Innocent III., the greatest of the
Popes and one of the best, to Arnold Amalric,
the greatest of the Abbots and onè of the worst.
In these letters, closely contemporary with the
romance of the Graal, these relations are defined

by Scriptural analogies from the Old Testament and the New. The Pope is Aaron, the High Priest of the Temple. The Abbot is Moses, the Captain of the armies of God. The Pope is the successor of Peter, the Apostle of the Church of the Circumcision. The Abbot is the successor of Paul, the Apostle of the Church of the Gentiles. No illustrations could more aptly define the commanding position held at the time by the Abbot of Cîteaux.

But this was not all. The predominance of the Evangelical party in the Church of England at the time of Negro emancipation, or even of the Puritans in the days of Cromwell, was only a feeble reflection of the predominance of what may be called Cistercianism in the Church at this period. The claims of the Cistercians to superior sanctity, always proclaimed by their preaching, and not unfrequently justified by their practice, were admitted as unquestionable within, and very frequently without, the 'religious world' of the period. Kings and queens, and a vast array of minor nobilities, vied with each other in their benefactions to the Order, and even Emperors were fain to pass into the unknown world clad in the Cistercian habit, proof against the claws of the Evil One.

Yet more. The world, it was well known,

was beginning to 'verge on Antichrist and
Doom.' Joachim, Abbot of Flora in Calabria,
was a prophet whose utterances were not less
divinely inspired than those of Merlin, Rabanus,
or the Sibyls. To him it had been revealed
that the world should pass through three stages :
the first under the more direct governance of
God the Father, the second under that of God
the Son, and the third under that of God
the Holy Spirit. Each stage must have its own
Chosen People. In the first they had been the
Children of Israel. In the second they had
been the disciples of Christ. In the third it
needed no argument to prove that the Chosen
People were the Order of Cîteaux. The
stages overlapped by considerable periods, but
the transition from one to another was defined
by some critical event. At one time Joachim
thought that this event would take place in the
year 1200, and that the government of the
world would then pass into the hands of the
Third Person of the Holy Trinity in a manner
that none could mistake or deny. He was
certain that Antichrist had already been born
into the world. He seems to have lived long
enough to find that the millennium did not
commence with the year 1200, and to adjourn
the verification of his predictions to 1260, a year

much fancied by later interpreters of prophecy. These were not the idle dreams of an unheeded visionary. They were accepted as revelations of the Everlasting Gospel by all the Cistercians and their friends. Even Innocent could speak a kindly word in season for the Calabrian seer, and a slight taint of peradventure heresy only gave zest to the appetite of the numberless mystics of that age of mysticism.

At this time, then, when the Abbot of Cîteaux was recognised as leader and chief of the most influential organisation in Christendom, more actively influential than either Papacy or Empire, when Innocent had proclaimed him Moses, and the armies of the Albigensian Crusade hailed him as General-in-Chief, the romancer was amply justified in calling him King and making him brother of the Emperor and Pope. Whether the ' Lower Folk,' the *basse gent*, refers to the monastic brethren of the Order under his rule, or to the actual lay-troops and knights of the crusading army he commanded, may perhaps be doubtful. There is no doubt that the third uncle of Perceval is Arnold Amalric, Abbot of Cîteaux, or his successor; the second, King Fisherman, Pope Innocent III., or his successor Honorius III.; and the first, the King of

Castle Mortal, the Emperor Otho iv., or Frederic ii.

Who, then, is Perceval? He is a son of the Church and the Church's champion against the Albigenses, Alain de l'Isle. Obviously, therefore, he is an ecclesiastical hero. He is no lay-knight, noble or otherwise. He is to be sought not among the kings or captains of the age, but among the saints of the Church. His knighthood is spiritual, not temporal. Yet a knight he is throughout—according to the romance, the Best Knight in the World. His sonship to Alain suggests that he may be a champion of the Church engaged in the Albigensian Crusade. The romancer gives us his portrait: 'Good knight was he without fail, for he was chaste and virgin of his body, and hardy of heart and puissant . . . not boastful was he of speech, and it seemed not by his cheer that he had so great courage.' Other touches are added later. He is secret in his ways. He is true and loving to his friends, but the vengeance he wreaks upon his enemies knows neither pity nor remorse. Readers of Dante will already have surmised his identity. Bonaventura in Paradise describes him to the poet. He is 'the amorous wooer of the Christian faith, the holy athlete, kindly to his own, and harsh to his enemies,' who 'smote the stocks of heresy with a blow that fell keenest where the resistance was most stubborn,' the vinedresser in the vineyard of the Lord, who, possessing him wholly, willed also that he should be called 'the Lord's own,' Dominic.

It is even so. Perceval, the Saint of romance, is none other than Dominic, the Knight of the Church. Strange and startling, almost paradoxical, as the collocation of names and the ideas connected with them may be, the close and vital analogy between the champion of the court of Arthur and the champion of the court of Innocent is more than likeness—it is identity. Not a single 'note' of personal appearance, temperament, intellect, or character recorded in the lives of the saint but is faithfully reproduced in the hero of the romance. He has exchanged what the old author calls 'the armour of religion' for the armour of knighthood, and that is all. He is the same man. If these few identifications are correct, they cannot but help to unravel no small portion of the mystery in which the romance is enshrouded.

A more illogical foundation for a story than that of the romance it would be hard to conceive. A young unknown knight comes to the court of a great king, where a strange and holy mystery passes before him. Because he does not then and there demand to be told the meaning of the mystery, the flood-gates of disaster are lifted on Greater Britain and the world at large, and the King himself is smitten with a mysterious malady which in course of time brings him to his grave. No wilder enigma, it is safe to say, was ever propounded to his readers by the writer of any religious novel. Yet the author of the Book of the Graal evidently takes it for granted that the amazing postulate on which his phantasmagory is founded will be accepted as strictly in accordance with the nature of things and the established order of the universe. In the world of which he writes, the fatal ailments of monarchs, illimitable civil war and desolation of kingdoms, are the natural and inevitable results of the shyness of a young military gentleman, who refrains from making inquiries which he feels might be regarded as impertinent. It is most unfortunate, but so it is, and under the existing conditions in this strange world cannot be otherwise.

At first sight, indeed, it seems as if little were gained by substituting Dominic for

Perceval and Pope Innocent III. for King Fisherman. It is only in the pages of romance that Innocent takes to his bed because Dominic does not ask questions, or that unheard-of calamities fall upon England for the same fantastic reason. Still, authors of spiritual romances have at times a strange way of putting things. When they chronicle events, they do not use the language of the chroniclers. History wears a different aspect in the spiritual world. A heavy blow to the influence of the Church, for instance, would be likely enough to appear in religious romance as a malady inflicted on the Head of the Church. A far-reaching spiritual calamity in England or elsewhere would almost certainly be described as a desolation of the kingdom. The problem to be solved, in fact, reduces itself to a sum in historic proportion. As King Fisherman is to the Pope, or S. Dominic to Sir Perceval, so is the malady of King Fisherman or the Desolation of England to the real event recorded.

Up to this point all that can be predicated about these events is that they resulted from some error of omission on the part of Dominic when on a visit to the Court of Innocent at Rome at some period before the events recorded in the story are supposed to have taken place. Dominic paid only one well-authenticated visit to Rome before the year 1215, and it is on this first visit that he must have exercised his gift of reticence with such disastrous results. The date of the visit is probably 1204, although some of Dominic's biographers relegate it to the next year. All, however, are agreed as to the main circumstances in which it took place. In 1203, Alphonso the Noble, King of Castile, was anxious to find a suitable spouse for his eldest son Ferdinand, then a lad of thirteen. He accordingly sent an embassy to the father of 'a certain noble lady of the Marches' to request her hand in marriage. The envoys returned with a favourable answer, and were again despatched with a large retinue to bring the bride to Spain. The Lady of the Marches died before their arrival, and the ambassadors with their retinue turned aside to visit Rome on their way back to Castile.

The chief of the embassy was Diego d'Azeveda, Bishop of Osma in Old Castile, who had brought with him as companion and lieutenant Dominic, sub-prior of the Canons of the same see. Dominic at this time was a man of thirty-three, well known in his own scholastic and canonical circles for his eloquence, devotion, and austere purity of life. On their way to the 'Marches,' wherever they may have been, the Spaniards found themselves at Toulouse, where Dominic was lodged in the house of a heretic. Most of the night was spent in earnest converse, and before the morrow dawned the heretic had renounced his heresy. Dominic accepted the omen. The idea which dominated his life, the foundation of an Order of Preachers, had already flashed across the thoughts of others besides Dominic. Here was the divine call to devote himself body and soul to its realisation. A tragic end had cut short the temporal mission of the Bishop and his sub-prior. Both felt that a higher Power than any King of Castile had now charged them with a spiritual mission of far deeper moment to the world and to King Fisherman at Rome.

The self-imposed mission was to confer with the spiritual monarch of Christendon on a New Way of dealing with the heathen and the heretic. They reached Rome, still accompanied by their Castilian retinue, apparently in the spring or early summer of 1204, and were at once cordially and even affectionately received by Innocent. The New Way they had to

propose, so far as it can be deduced from the
subsequent conduct of the envoys, was entirely
admirable as regards the first step to be taken
in reference to the heretics, and entirely
detestable as regards the last. Dominic had
felt the irrefragable force of one favourite
argument of the Albigenses. 'See,' said they,
'how these noble knights of Christ on horse-
back go about to teach us poor folk on foot!
How bravely Dives preaches to Lazarus the
Gospel of Him who was poor and rejected of
men!' Dominic's answer was worthy of a
saint: 'Let them that preach to this people
go among them barefoot in the spirit of
humility, the spirit of Christ. Let them be
themselves beggars, and bear the good tidings
of a crucified Saviour to Lazarus at the gate,
clad like Lazarus in misery and rags.'

Such was the New Way, and so far, it was
worthy of all acceptation. But when the
preaching was done, what then? For them
that renounced their heresy, public penance,
ignominy, or exile—for them that refused to
renounce, the sword, the halter, or the stake.
In these respects, the New Way was as the
old. To justify the system, not to reform or
abolish it, was the object of Diego, Dominic,
and Innocent. 'You slaughter and burn us,'

cried the heretics, 'for not accepting the truth
as it is in Christ. How can we accept Christ's
truth if you do not preach it to us as Christ
preached?' Dominic's answer is: 'We admit
the justice of your plea. Henceforth we will
preach as Christ preached. If you still harden
your hearts against the truth, we shall be justified in the eyes of man and God in destroying
you utterly. As righteously will men burn
your bodies here on earth as God will hereafter
burn your souls in hell.'

At the time this new scheme was laid before
Innocent, he was ready to welcome any
suggestion for dealing with heresy in
Languedoc that promised even a temporary
break in the perennial monotony of failure that
for generations had attended every effort of the
Church in the land of the troubadour. The
New Way and the new men should at least
have a fair trial. Diego was anxious to make
the first experiment of the system on the
Comans, just then the heathens most in
evidence, whose country lay on the shores of
the Black Sea. Dominic asked to be allowed
to try it on the heretics in the neighbourhood
of Toulouse. Innocent sided with the Sub-
prior rather than the Bishop. He decided that
the energies of both, instead of being dispersed

by separation, should be made doubly effective
by union ; and further, that the trial of the
New Way should be made in conjunction with
the efforts of the legates and preachers then at
work against heresy in Languedoc. Diego
was granted leave of absence from the see of
Osma till the end of 1206. Both were to
undergo a brief apprenticeship to the methods
of the Old Way at Cîteaux before entering
on their missionary labours. Both were to
exercise authority as holding a commission
direct from Innocent ; but both were to be
under the command of Arnold, Abbot of
Cîteaux, and his fellow-legates *in partibus.*

The plan of campaign was evidently carefully arranged. First of all, the new system
was to be launched in a public manner which
could hardly fail to commend it to popular
sympathy and enthusiasm. Preaching by barefoot preachers under vows of poverty, chastity,
and obedience was to be carried on for two
years at least, and every effort should be made
to conciliate the heretics. They should be
invited to confer, discuss, and deliberate.
Severe measures should for a time remain in
abeyance. The Gospel should be preached as
Christ preached it. If at the end of the allotted
time the heretics still continued obstinately

unconverted, the last argument of the Church no less than of kings should then be employed. The syllogism was not strikingly logical, but it was sometimes effective. The major premiss was that it is the duty of the Church to extirpate heresy. The minor premiss was that it is the duty of the Secular Arm to assist her so to do. The conclusion was that if the Secular Arm failed to do so, it was the duty of the Church to transfer the Secular power from the temporal ruler unwilling or unable to assist the Church to another temporal ruler who both could and would. In actual practice, the major took the form of Interdict, the minor of Crusade, the conclusion of a decree of deposition.

Interdict as an ecclesiastical weapon has long been obsolete, and the part it once played in both civil and religious history has been very generally misunderstood. It must have held a foremost place among the topics discussed by Innocent with his Spanish visitors before they started on their mission into Languedoc. The very air of Christendom was dark with Interdict. The one aim of the new preachers was to persuade the heretics to attend the ministrations of the Church. The efficacy of Interdict depended on its suspending those ministrations. Some kind of arrangement by which the exercise of the power of Interdict could be so limited and controlled as not to interfere too seriously with the practical work of the preachers was a necessity of the case. Interdict of the heretical country, pure and simple, would have been the very suicide of orthodoxy. A certain simple-minded bishop who was among the first to try the experiment of interdicting the Holy Sacrifice throughout his diocese, had been surprised to find that 'the people were none the better' for the infliction. Two centuries later, in the days of Innocent, the pontiffs and prelates who followed the example were under no such hallucination. None knew better than they that Interdict could never tend to godliness of life or the welfare of souls. Innocent freely employed it as a means of coercing powerful delinquents whom it was impossible or impolitic to attempt to coerce otherwise, but neither he nor any of the best of his predecessors ever regarded its exercise as other than a hateful resource only justifiable in the absence of any less objectionable alternative. Ample proof of this is to be found in the many privileges granted by many successive Popes to certain religious Orders for the special object of mitigating some of the

worst evils and hardships which the sentence
inevitably entailed.

Among these Orders, that of the Cistercians
naturally held a foremost place, as being at the
time the real political executive of the Papacy.
Among the many favours granted by Eugenius
III. to his old friend and preceptor Bernard, the
second and greater founder of the Cistercian
Order, may be reckoned the charter of privileges granted to the Order in 1152, and
signed by no less than fourteen cardinals as
well as the Pope. The thirteenth article of
this memorable document runs thus :—

'This also hath our sanction, that none of
your churches shall be compelled to abstain
from divine offices on account of any General
Interdict ; but in time of Interdict it shall be
lawful for the Cistercians, excommunicated and
interdicted persons having been ejected and
the doors closed, in a low voice to celebrate
the Divine solemnities.'

This privilege, granted in later years to
several other Orders, had at the beginning
of the thirteenth century become the common property of the great majority of the
regular as distinct from the secular clergy. In
Languedoc, however, before the propaganda
had been reinforced by the arrival of Diego

and Dominic, it had been found necessary at once to modify the right to inflict the sentence of Interdict, and to confer on the Cistercians a far wider privilege of which they enjoyed an absolute monopoly.

II

GAWAIN

Ad un occaso quasi ed ad un orto
  Bugea siede e la terra ond' io fui,
Che fe del sangue suo gia caldo il porto.
  Folco mi disse quella gente, a cui
Fu noto il nome mio; e questo cielo
  Di me s'impronta, com' io fe di lui.

(PARADISO, IX.)

THE Albigensian Crusade, like the French
Revolution, is a hideous sequence of crimes
against humanity. Like the Revolution, it is
also much more. It must be remembered that
a large proportion, probably a large majority,
of the Albigensian heretics did really hold
doctrines at least as incompatible with morality
and social civilisation as those of the Mormons,
though in a diametrically opposite direction.
Carried into practice in the England of to-day,
such doctrines would bring their professors
into immediate collision with the police and
law courts, the gaol and the lunatic asylum.
The methods actually adopted against them

were the methods of the thirteenth century; but
the suppression of heresy of the kind by some
method or other would be as necessary to the
community to-day or to-morrow as in any
yesterday of civilised life. The non-Walden-
sian heresies, indeed, could only have thriven
as they did in a community of low social
organisation. They found a congenial home
in 'Le Midi,' a kingdom without a king, a
country without a name, a territory without
a frontier, a people without a nationality.
'Languedoc' and 'the Albigenses' are mere
approximate definitions.

As early as April 1198, Innocent had com-
menced the operations against the heretics of
Languedoc which culminated in the Albigensian Crusade. He sent a Legate, Rayner, into
the 'infected' provinces with a chosen band of
colleagues, urgently commending him to all
the spiritual and temporal authorities who
could render any assistance. The Interdict
difficulty had pressed hardly on former lega-
tions against the heretics. Innocent now cut
the knot by delegating to Rayner absolute power
of excommunication and interdict in the parts
to which he was accredited; and not only was
this power confided to the Legate, but the
further privilege of disregarding any sentence

of excommunication or interdict pronounced by any other authority whatsoever save only Innocent himself. There had been many changes in the Legation since the first mission of Rayner; and at the time Diego and Dominic were conferring with Innocent, Arnold of Cîteaux was the acting chief, with Peter of Castelnau and Rayner, both also Cistercians, as his colleagues. But any changes which had been made in the system pursued were in favour of enlarging rather than retrenching the privileges both of the Legation and the Order. Practically the absolute power of dealing with the heretics was in the hands of the Cistercians; and in talking over the general state of affairs in Languedoc, it was hardly likely that Diego or Dominic would inquire very curiously into the distinction between the privileges granted to the Cistercians generally and those specially granted to the Cistercian Legation then militant in Languedoc. Still less probable was it that either of them would ask for the extension of the special privileges enjoyed by the Legation to the Order generally. Doubtless, had such a contingency as the great English Interdict been in contemplation at the time, they would have suggested that if the sins of King John against the Church demanded the suspension of divine service and of the administration of the Sacraments throughout the country, at least the Order specially intrusted with the task of preaching the Gospel should be allowed under certain conditions to continue its ministrations and be free to fulfil its special functions in its own way. Had such a suggestion been made at this time, it is clear from Innocent's own distinct declarations in after days that the boon would not have been refused. But Innocent was not asked. The Albigensians and the Albigensian Legation were uppermost in the minds of all present; and, as regarded these, all difficulties in case of Interdict had already been removed. A remote future contingency under altered conditions was most unlikely to suggest itself as demanding immediate attention. Perceval left the Castle-Palace of King Fisherman, and the momentous question of Cistercian privilege in case of Interdict, discussed and settled long since in the case of Languedoc, was left undiscussed and unsettled in the case of any other country. The question to whom the Graal should be served remained unasked. A few short years, and all England, all the Cistercian Order throughout the world, would be plunged into lamentation and mourning and woe because of the missed opportunity. The 'one little word' had not been spoken, and 'thereby happened such mischance in Greater Britain that all the land fell into sore sorrow.'

A careful reader of the ' High History ' will perhaps note that the question which Perceval omitted to ask is presented under two phases. He is rebuked apparently not only for not having asked *unto whom* the Graal is served, but also *whereof* it served. The first question in the mouth of Dominic would, I apprehend, have taken, if it had been asked, a form of this kind : ' In time of Interdict, will it be lawful for the Cistercians to celebrate mass, and to administer the Holy Sacrament to such as they may consider worthy ? ' The second question has reference to the Sacrament itself, but in special connection with the method of dealing with the heretics of Languedoc. The dogma of Transubstantiation was not declared *de Fide* until the Lateran Council of 1215. It had, however, been steadily growing into favour ever since the days of Hildebrand and Paschasius Radbert ; and by the time that Innocent ascended the Papal throne, had commended itself to general acceptance by the faithful. Technically, therefore, it was still possible before 1215 to hold views at variance with the dogma without necessarily being heretical. It followed that those who held such views could not legally be convicted of heresy and handed over to the Secular Arm for punishment as heretics unless they were also guilty in some other respect. Now, some considerable number of the Waldenses—always to be carefully distinguished from the Albigenses —seem to have held, nominally at least, all the doctrines of the Church with the one exception of Transubstantiation. What was to be done with them ? Had Dominic asked the question in this concrete form and obtained a reply, he would have saved himself a good deal of trouble and the commission, apparently, of a good deal of illegality. Innocent seems to have been urged more than once by others to make an authoritative declaration on the subject ; but his answer was always that he intended shortly to call a General Council which would decide the matter definitively in the name of the Church. Meanwhile, he did not conceal his own opinion, but simply left each case in which the question arose to be dealt with by those whose duty it was to deal with it. It is easy to see how the two questions came to be confused in the mind of a Cistercian romancer who was weaving into his romance the history of both the Albigensian Crusade and the English Interdict. The real

omission of Dominic in the eyes of the romancer
and the Cistercians generally was not so much
his not asking this question or that, but neglect-
ing so favourable an opportunity of coming to
a clear understanding with Innocent as to the
Mass and its celebration generally. Had he
done so, it would materially have lightened
the labours of the Legation in Languedoc; it
would still more materially have mitigated the
horrors of the Interdict in England.

The history of the Albigensian Crusade itself
lies beside my present purpose; but its close
connection with the English Interdict has never
received the attention it deserves, and a sketch
of the events that led up to it may assist
towards a clearer understanding of both events.
In the early spring of 1205, Dominic, Diego,
and their royal Castilian retinue left Rome for
Citeaux to be initiated into Cistercian ways, if
not into the Order itself. Not for nothing did
they travel in pomp for the last time. Their
progress through Genoa and Turin and over the
passes of the Alps and the Jura into Burgundy
announced that they were authorised envoys
not so much of the King of Castile as of the
Holy See, and that their mission was of moment
to all the temporal and spiritual powers in
Christendom. Whether the Abbey of Cîteaux

was burdened with the entertainment of the
escort does not appear, but the brotherhood
certainly could not fail to be impressed by
the imposing dignity of their Spanish visitors
arriving in such state from the Castle of King
Fisherman. The guests on their part were
delighted with Cîteaux. Everything was en-
chanting except the absence of Abbot Arnold,
who had at that particular juncture retired for
a short time from his duties as Legate in
Languedoc to implore help against the heretics
from King Philip 'Augustus' in Paris. Diego,
always enthusiastic and effusive, insisted on
donning the habit of the Order forthwith.
Dominic, not less enthusiastic, but more re-
strained, preferred not to bind himself to a new
obedience which might embarrass his action in
the future. After a stay of some weeks, during
which both were duly instructed in manners
and customs Cistercian, they continued their
princely progress southward to Montpelier.
The headquarters of the Legation against the
heretics were just now at Castelnau, the old
Sustantion, some two miles outside the city, a
stronghold belonging to the family of Peter of
Castelnau, Archdeacon of Maguelonne, one of
the three legates now in charge. His colleagues
were Brother Ralph, Abbot of Fontfroid,

and Arnold of Cîteaux himself, just returned
from his conference with Philip.

All three were sorely depressed—spiritless,
baffled, and beaten. More than two years
Peter and Ralph had laboured in vain. They
had summoned Raymond of Toulouse to expel
the heretics. They had made the capitouls of
Toulouse swear to maintain the Catholic faith.
They had suspended the Bishop of Beziers.
They had accused Berenger, Archbishop of
Narbonne, of negligence, and had made him
disgorge the most scandalous of his pluralities.
But, as against the heretics they were none the
forwarder, and wrote earnestly to Innocent
requesting him to relieve them of their hopeless
legation. Innocent refused, and urged them
to new efforts, sending Arnold, then lately
elected Abbot of Cîteaux, as a colleague. The
'Secular Arm' was again invoked. Peter II.
of Arragon was at the time overlord of half
Montpelier, Innocent himself being overlord
of the other half. Peter was accordingly called
on to assist the legates, and Innocent assured
him free sovereignty over all the territory he
could win by force of arms from heretic lords.
Peter accordingly took the Castle of Lescure
from an Albigensian noble, but showed himself
lukewarm in the matter of general persecution ;

and before Innocent issued a commission consisting of the Bishop of Pampeluna and the three legates to inquire into a matrimonial suit pending between Peter and his wife Mary of Montpelier (June 1206), all hope of finding him an efficient champion of orthodoxy had been abandoned.

Philip of France, wariest of European diplomatists, save Innocent himself, was still wroth with Innocent for upholding, by a long interdict on his country, his marriage with Ingebiorg of Denmark. The refusal of a divorce had been the death of Agnes of Meran, the only woman that Philip had really loved. After her death, Innocent had hastened to legitimate her children, but his wise and courageous resolution to lend no countenance to royal adultery rankled, and continued to rankle, in Philip's heart. Still, Philip was statesman as well as lover. His quarrel with Innocent was personal. If Innocent could only appeal strongly enough to his ambition —and the creation of a larger united France was surely no ignoble ambition—Philip might consent to co-operate with him in abolishing heresy from Languedoc.

The object of Arnold's conference with Philip was to renew and strengthen an offer

made more than once before. If Philip would
only send an army to invade *Le Midi* and lend
the legates the assistance of his powerful
‘ Secular Arm ’ in extirpating heresy, he should
be free to annex the whole of the conquered
territory to the crown of France with Innocent’s hearty goodwill. If he himself cannot
come, let him send his son. Only let heresy
be extinguished, and no hindrance to the temporal aggrandisement of France will be offered
by the Papacy. His armies shall enjoy all the
indulgences and privileges granted to crusaders
against the Saracen ; and as all the existing
temporal princes in the ‘ infected ’ provinces
will be declared excommunicate and deposed,
he need have no scruple as sovereign in invading the lands of his vassals. Every argument, we may be sure, in favour of immediate
armed interference, was urged by Arnold on the
King’s attention. Philip, we may be equally
sure, saw that Languedoc could be annexed to
France at a cheaper rate. Arnold returned
discomfited to his colleagues. Before they
were joined by Diego and Dominic, they had
once more written to Innocent in despair,
petitioning to be released from the legation.

A council of war was held with the new-
comers the day after their arrival. The legates

stated their case, and pointed out the insuperable difficulty of converting the heretics until the 'Secular Arm' could be healed of its inveterate palsy. It was Diego d'Azeveda's turn to speak; and the manner of his coming, no less than the letters he brought from Innocent, invested his speech with an authority that even three legates could not lightly gainsay. 'You legates,' said he, 'begin at the wrong end. You come to your work swaggering on your tall horses followed by bedizened footmen as if you were so many princes of the blood. Look at these damnable heretics! With their fair-seeming poverty and humility they beat you all hollow! How can it be otherwise? Meet them with their own weapons! It is not preaching, but practice, that converts to the truth!' It was probably Arnold of Cîteaux who was first to grasp the irony of the situation. 'That is all very well, my Lord Bishop, but how about this gallant cavalcade of your own?—these footmen in the courtyard, these horses in the stables? We are quite at one with you as to the priceless worth of example, but what are we to do —here and now?' 'Do?' retorts Diego; 'do as I do!' Out he strides forthwith to summon the whole company of retainers, knights and squires, cooks, sergeants, and grooms, and packs them off bag and baggage, horse and foot and sumpter mule. 'Back to Castile, every mother's son of you. Bear loyal and humble greeting to my Lord the King, and tell him his servants are minded as for the next two years at least to go on foot preaching to the poor, even as Christ preached, on the hither side the mountains!' The hour has come. The 'New Way' has been inaugurated by a symbolic ceremony worthy of the influence it is hereafter to exercise on human destinies. The first friar has made his entrance on the world's stage. Dominic has set his hand to the work under the protection of Cîteaux. Perceval has taken his new shield from Arthur's court. Dominic will fight in loyal comradeship with Cîteaux, but will never become Cistercian. Perceval will fight for Arthur, but never take his seat at the Table Round.

It was July when the new preachers joined the legates. In the middle of September Arnold had to be back at Cîteaux to preside over the Annual Chapter of the Order. Innocent sent a letter to the united brethren on this occasion, which may perhaps have lingered in the memory of the romancer when he bestowed the title of King Fisherman on the occupant of the Roman See. 'Ever since we were raised by the call of the Lord to the office of Fisherman, we have piloted over the sea the bark intrusted to us so as to loose our net, according to the word of the Lord, for the taking of fishes. But this great and spacious sea, lashed by the roaring of a most pitiless storm, hath begun to surge against our bark in billows so many and so huge, that not only are we somewhat hindered from following our craft of fishing, but the control and steering of the bark have become well-nigh impossible. . . . Yet, albeit we were hemmed round with difficulties, we have been heedful to steer with such seamanship as we could, and now and again have so spread our fisherman's net in the sea as to enclose therein certain fish of no ordinary bigness. Nevertheless, what time we trusted to take them forth at the haven, sundry of them burst the net, and not only slipped away themselves forthwith into the bowels of the deep, but compelled others to slip back after them. . . . But what these things may be, most beloved sons, whereof we speak thus figura-tively, will not, we trust, be hidden from your prudence, so you exercise the keenness of your discreet consideration in searching them out narrowly. . . .'

It is a strained and strangely laboured parable

that King Fisherman sends as his message to
the Cistercian congress, but no great keenness
of discreet consideration is needed to interpret
these paragraphs. Peter of Arragon and Philip
of France were assuredly fish of no ordinary
bigness ; and both, to name no others, had just
slipped back into the bowels of the deep at the
moment he had thought to land them. But
the Fisherman does not despair. In concluding
his piscatory eclogue, he intimates that he
knows a fetch that will bring them all safe
home with a seine-net full of fish. Legate
Arnold must have enjoyed a good time when
he expounded the true inwardness of the message to the assembled Abbots, when he revealed
the secret of the New Way, and invited volun-
teers to join the standard of the new apostles.
He returned to Montpelier with twelve devoted
brethren of the Order, eager only to preach
the Gospel to the heretics as Christ had preached
it, barefoot and in rags. The Order of
Preachers was not formally instituted until
after the death of Innocent. It was already in
active existence.

Diego had promised to return to his bishopric
at Osma before the end of the year 1206.
It would seem from the actual sequence of
events that this was also the term fixed for

ending the trial of the New Way in Languedoc. Until that time, the interference of the Secular Arm should be welcome, indeed, but should not again be urgently invoked. The red right hand of vengeance should be stayed until the sinners had been allowed time to repent. After the truth had been preached as Christ preached it, Divine justice would be dealt out to the stiff-necked generation, and Christendom would hail with joy the doom that should fall on the faithless. The success of the preachers as regarded the Waldenses, though far from equalling their hopes, had been considerable. Their failure as against the Albigenses had been total and ignominious. Before starting homeward, Diego challenged the heretics to a final conference at Pamiers. It was held in the castle of Raymond Roger, Count of Foix, and was attended by Fulke, Bishop of Toulouse, Navarre of Conserans, and a troop of abbots, all anxious to cheer the departure of the apostle of the New Way by at least one decisive victory. Raymond Roger was a prominent heretic champion. His wife was a Waldensian, and of his two sisters, one was Waldensian, while the other, Esclarmonde, was a Catharist ' Perfect.' At the conference, Esclarmonde rose to speak. One of the new preachers, Brother

Stephen de Minia, interposed : 'Go, my Lady, to your distaff and spin ! No right have you to speak on these matters.' Diego 'prayed God to smite the heretics with His strong right hand, for never would they open their eyes till they had tasted of the cup of His wrath.'

The arbiter on this occasion was one of the secular clergy, Master Arnold de Campranhan, a friend of the Waldenses, and trusted in their camp. He and a large number of other Waldensians recanted their heretical tenets either at or immediately after the conference. Among them was Durand de Huesca, the founder of an orthodox Waldensian Order, if the communities established by him and others can be called an Order, within the pale of the Church, and under the special protection of Innocent. This was the last conference of the kind. At Pamiers, Diego was already on his way to Osma. Some of the preachers walked with the old man barefoot across the passes of the Pyrenees. He arrived at Osma wayworn and weary, in the last days of 1206, and died February 6, 1207.

Legate Ralph had died shortly before Diego's departure. Legate Arnold of Cîteaux was absent on a second mission to Philip Augustus, destined to be of incalculable historic moment.

Legate Peter of Castelnau found abundant occupation in harassing Raymond of Toulouse by the exercise of every ecclesiastical weapon of offence, personal excommunication, interdict of his dominions, declaration of Crusade. This last step was taken in November. Raymond quailed, again promised obedience to the legate's impossible demands, and summoned him to S. Gilles. Peter obeyed, but only for the purpose of adding insult to injury. After the interview, he and his companions left S. Gilles and passed the night in a village on the banks of the Rhone, intending to cross the river on the morrow. They were about to enter the ferry-boat after hearing mass in the morning, when a knight of the family of the Porcellets, retainers of Raymond, avenged the insult offered to his lord by running the legate through the body with a spear.

The murder took place on January 15, 1208. In the absence of Arnold, the legation in Languedoc was without a legate, and consequently shorn of more than half its authority. A meeting was held of all the remaining members of the legation, and it was decided to send two of their number at once to Rome to inform King Fisherman of the murder, and to urge the necessity of launching the crusade against

Raymond and his heretic subjects without a moment's further delay. The enterprise to the Castle of the Graal was forthwith joyously undertaken by Fulke, Bishop of Toulouse, and Navarre, Bishop of Conserans.

Fulke had been consecrated Bishop of Toulouse shortly before the arrival of Diego and Dominic, the three legates having deposed Raymond of Rabastens, the former bishop. By metropolitical right, the see of Toulouse was suffragan to the archbishopric of Narbonne. The legates, rightly considering Berenger of Narbonne scandalously unfitted for the post of Archbishop, had wrongfully caused Fulke to be consecrated by the Archbishop of Arles, a proceeding which sufficiently indicates the absolute power exercised at the time by the Cistercian champions in Languedoc. Fulke was a man with a history. His father, a wealthy Genoese merchant, died, leaving him a considerable fortune. Money-grubbing had no attractions for the youth in comparison with the *gai saber* ; and he made his first appearance on the world's stage as a gallant retainer of the viceregal court at Aix in Provence, at that time presided over by Raymond Barral of Marseilles, as Governor under Alphonso, the first Count of Provence, but the second King

of Arragon of that name. Raymond Barral of
Marseilles was the third of five brothers who
shared among them the viscounty of that city,
a viscounty originally created for a cadet of the
house of Provence. Neither he nor his wife
Azalais of Roquemartine, also a Porcellet,
and perhaps a sister of Peter's murderer, was
wealthy, and all the joint-viscounts in later
years agreed to sell their titles and rights to the
city of Marseilles, each receiving an annual
pension, a sum down, and the right to keep the
title for life. It has never been explained how
the young troubadour came by the title of
Fulke of Marseilles. It seems likely that it
really represents a money transaction between
Raymond Barral and himself. When Fulke
'entered religion,' the title may have reverted
to Raymond Barral, to be subsequently resold
to the city.

Be this as it may, Barral of Marseilles
became ' my good Lord ' to Fulke ; and Fulke,
as in troubadour duty bound, made poetic love,
possibly platonic, to Barral's wife Azalais.
The friendship between Barral and Fulke
seems to have remained unbroken. The lady,
however, either with or without reason, seems
to have waxed wroth with the poet, and he
certainly left Aix vowing never again to write

a line of verse. The gods have a kindly by-law relative to the broken oaths of poets and lovers, but the Monk of Montaudon insists on poking fun at the ' perjury ' of the ' merchant ' troubadour when he catches him rhyming again to another love. Before 1187, Fulke was received into the household of William of Montpelier ; and one of his poems is written at the command of the 'Empress,' to wit, Eudoxia, William's wife, who was repudiated by her husband in that year. Barral's wife Azalais died about the same time, and Fulke may have had a hand in bringing about Barral's second marriage with the infant Mary of Montpelier. It has been inferred from a poem he wrote in 1189, excusing Richard of England when he was excommunicated for not starting on the Crusade, that Fulke was at that time with Richard at Poitiers. The inference is perhaps too liberal from premisses so scanty. The same may be said of his alleged presence at Alarcos on July 18, 1195, when Alphonso ix. was defeated, and Christianity seemed on the eve of extinction in the Spanish peninsula. He certainly wrote a stirring *sirvente* on the occasion, but it affords no proof that he was himself one of the defeated warriors.

Shortly after this event, Fulke decided to

retire from the world and don the Cistercian habit. His old friends and patrons were dead. Troubadour life had palled on the passions of middle age. Religious sentiment was ripening into religious enthusiasm, and the humble penitence of the sinner, which inspired some of his noblest verses, was rapidly fermenting into the fanaticism of the persecutor. The century was drawing to a close, and the last days were at hand. Christendom was defeated in Syria and Spain, and the deadly cancer of heresy was eating into the very heart of the world. It was the eve of a new era. Fulke would fain devote his every faculty of body and soul to the extermination of the enemies of God. Even in that hour of darkness he knew no terror. It was not the darkness of coming night, but the darkness before the dawn.

It is at this point in Fulke's career that we hear for the first time of certain encumbrances not usually regarded as necessary to a trouba-dour—a legitimate wife and two sons. Who the lady may have been remains a mystery. There she was, and the only honourable means of getting rid of her was to send her to a nunnery. Perhaps she too desired nothing better. At any rate, father, mother, and sons all entered the 'religion' of Cîteaux; and in

January 1197, Fulke was able to sign himself Abbot of Thoronet, a Cistercian foundation in the diocese of Frejus.

In the year 1300, in the sphere of human love purified and hallowed, between Cunizza da Romano and Rahab the harlot, Dante saw and spoke with the beatified spirit of Fulke of Marseilles. Cunizza pointed him out to the poet with a true prophecy. The year that fulfils a century shall five times return, and the fame of the troubadour who renounced the earthly for the heavenly love shall still be remembered. Even such glory, she said, awaiteth him that on suchwise striveth after excellence, and entering on a new life leaveth the sinful life behind him for ever. Even before his name is spoken, Dante recognises that radiant joy of the third heaven glittering like a balass-ruby in the sun for the gladness that is in him ; for even as smiles are born on earth, so in heaven is brightness born of delight.

Petrarca also beheld his spirit in vision, but the vision is of the troubadour, not of the beatified minister of divine judgment. Folchetto— Petrarca may use the 'diminutive of affection' —is one of the slaves that wait upon the Triumph of Love. He marches captive between Giraud de Borneilh and Geoffry

D

Rudel of Blaye, the Pilgrim of Love, in the troop of Provençal singers headed by Arnaud d'Aniel. But Petrarca knows his greatness and his repentance. It is he who took from Genoa and gave to Marseilles the glory of his name —who thus symbolically exchanged his habit and his life, and became a citizen of the nobler fatherland.

This is the man, amorous, courteous, and chivalrous, past master in the art and mystery of love, long versed in the ways of the court and the camp, yet burning with the devout zeal of a convert, who has now emprised his way to the Castle of the Graal to confer with King Fisherman. Those who know Sir Gawain in all the earlier legends of the Graal will, like Dante, have recognised him before his name is spoken. Those who only know Sir Gawain in the later and ignobler legends will understand how such a character would be smirched and sullied when touched by the adulterous finger of the baser age.

III

KING FISHERMAN

Nove remus speciei
Rete novum datur ei.
Forma navis alia ;
Nam si remus celi clavis
Rete verbum, Petri navis
Presens est Ecclesia.

(Attributed to ADAM of S. VICTOR.)

AT the time Fulke arrived in Rome on his mission from Languedoc, affairs in England might well have suggested the expediency of extending the privileges enjoyed by the Cistercian legation in *Le Midi* to the Order in Greater Britain. After the death of Hubert, Archbishop of Canterbury in 1205, a majority of the monks of Christchurch had elected their sub-prior to the vacant see. King John, the bishops-suffragan of the province, and the dissentient brethren of the convent, elected John de Gray, Bishop of Norwich, to the primacy. Innocent, for valid reasons in both cases, had set aside both elections; and, after some fruitless correspondence with John on the subject, consecrated Stephen Langton, Cardinal-priest of S. Chrysogonus, Archbishop of Canterbury at Viterbo on June 17, 1207. John refused to allow Langton to set foot in England, drove out the monks of Christchurch, quartered a troop of soldiers in their cloisters, and confiscated their broad lands to the Crown. Innocent in vain implored John to accept the new Archbishop. John was obdurate. Innocent threatened excommunication and interdict. John swore by the teeth of God, and indulged in one of those fits of maniac fury which the sons of Eleanor believed that they inherited from a veritable she-demon of the Pit, wooed and won by an ancestral Count of Guienne. It was the one inheritance that John knew how to keep.

On August 25, 1207, Innocent had appointed three bishops—William of London, Eustace of Ely, and Malger of Worcester—to act as Commissioners of Interdict. They were to exhort John to accept Stephen as Archbishop, and to show him due reverence and honour. If he still refused, they were to promulgate a sentence of interdict forbidding all offices of religion, save only the baptism of infants, and shrift for the dying. If even this infliction does not bring him to his senses, Innocent adds : 'We will take heed to make heavy our hands against him.' In November the letters had been issued declaring the Albigensian Crusade, and calling on Philip Augustus, as well as all dukes, counts, knights, and the faithful generally, to assist the Church in the extirpation of heresy. All the goods and belongings of the crusaders were taken under the direct protection of the Holy See. All indulgences granted to other crusaders were extended to those willing to take arms against the heretics, and all crusaders who could seize were entitled to hold the lands of any heretic lord. At the very same time—the letters are dated the next day—the Interdict Commissioners had been strictly enjoined to promulgate the Interdict throughout England and Wales, and a notable addition had been made to their instructions. All the churches of all the Orders, even those of the Hospitallers and Templars, were to be included in the Interdict. No exception was to be made in favour of the Cistercians or any other. No privilege was to be allowed to the regular clergy any more than to the secular.

This difference in the methods adopted in the

two cases is indeed signal. In Languedoc, the
Cistercians had been allowed a free hand in the
matter of Interdict, and had exercised it with
absolutely despotic independence. In England,
not only had the whole conduct and management
of the Interdict been transferred from the Cistercians to a body of Episcopal Commissioners, but
the Cistercians had been denied even their usual
privileges in times of Interdict. The pheno-
menon is strange, but far enough from being
inscrutable. For years past, Aaron at Rome
had felt that Moses at Cîteaux was encroaching
perilously on his prerogatives. The executive
of the Papacy was gradually supplanting the
Papacy itself. Innocent was not the man to
allow himself to become a *Roi fainéant* while
Arnold, Mayor of the Palace, usurped the real
sovereignty. More than once or twice already
he had remonstrated with Arnold on the
subject of his high-handed proceedings, and
had asserted his own right to dictate the line
of policy, if not the practical measures, to be
adopted. At this moment the two were in
direct conflict on a vital question of European
politics. Philip Augustus of France, following
in his father's footsteps, had devoted himself
to the noble ambition — none the less noble
because the means employed were at times

ignoble — of creating a greater and united
France. The full realisation of his idea would
have been to transfigure the comparatively
petty territory he had inherited into an Empire
mightier than that of Charlemagne, and the
Kings of France into Emperors of Christendom, the monarchs of the temporal world,
as the Pope was of the spiritual. But Philip
was above all things a practical statesman.
His methods were businesslike, and his policy
that of prosaic common-sense. The murder
of Prince Arthur by his uncle King John of
England had afforded him an excellent opportunity of carrying out his long-cherished
intention of annexing Normandy and much
besides to the crown of France. The next
question was, In which direction lay the most
promising prospect of extending his frontiers?
Languedoc was not a matter of pressing importance. In a vague and nominal way, it was
already mostly a French fief. Its geographical
situation and the natural course of events would
inevitably sooner or later make it an integral part
of the French kingdom. But England? Was
a more favourable opportunity of invading
England itself likely to occur? John was
rich, but that was all. He could no more
hold England against a determined attack by

Philip than he had held Normandy. He was a convicted murderer, and the seizure of his lands would be applauded by the sense of justice of all Christendom.

Abbot Arnold of Cîteaux, when he left his colleagues in Languedoc, had a tempting offer to lay before Philip: 'Help us to extirpate the heretics in Languedoc, and we will help you to conquer England.' The temptation was irresistible. To enlist the Cistercian brotherhood on his side was to forestall success. They counted for much more than an army. They would be an assurance to the world that the Church and righteousness itself were on the side of Philip. For the time-being, Philip believed that in securing the services of Arnold of Cîteaux he had secured the influence of Innocent. Arnold believed that in securing the secular arm of Philip, he had secured the victory of the Church in Languedoc, and that he had compromised Innocent beyond escape in case he should prove recalcitrant. The result of the compact between the French King and the King of the Lower Folk is writ large in the Albigensian Crusade and the twin-crusade against John of England led by Philip's son Lewis.

Meanwhile, both were reckoning without their host. Innocent's policy was not the

policy of either. He, too, was anxious that
France, the Eldest Son of the Church, should
be strong ; but at this time, at least, he had no
mind that the Empire should be transferred to
France. He had acquiesced, probably with
satisfaction, in the transfer of Normandy to
France. He desired that *Le Midi* should
become a part of the French kingdom. He
would have raised no objection to Philip's
absorbing all the continental possessions of the
kings of England. He drew his line where
Nature had drawn hers—along the 'silver
streak.' At a later day, sore against his will,
he found himself compelled to sanction the
project of an English invasion, but he soon had
reason to repent the false step he had taken ;
and his successful effort to retrace it and undo
the mischief he had done deserves, though it
is far enough from ever having received, the
gratitude of England. These events, however,
are still in the future. At present, his prime
object is to check the growth of Cistercian
predominance. Arnold's insubordination had
already verged closely on mutiny. It was high
time to read him a lesson in obedience.

When Fulke was at Rome, if any question
were to be asked of Innocent in reference to
the extension of Cistercian privileges, there was

obviously no time to lose. It was then or never.
Already it was too late to ask for the control
of the Interdict to be committed to the Cistercians. It was not too late to ask that their
privileges in regard to the celebration of Mass
should be respected. It can well be understood
that the Cistercian brethren in Rome would
urge upon Fulke the necessity of asking the
momentous question; well understood that
they should feel warmly indignant with Fulke
when he refrained from asking it. But 'the
Master of the Knights' may summon him
by word of mouth to put the question to the
damsels of the Graal. Gawain forgets, and
the desolation falls upon the kingdom of
Logres.

The murder or martyrdom of Peter of
Castelnau precipitated the measures long contemplated against John of England no less than
those against Raymond of Toulouse. Raymond
had married a Plantagenet among his many
other wives, the sister of John of England;
but the connection between the two potentates
was closer than that of a mere former union
between the families dictated by political expediency. They were not only on terms of
intimate friendship, but they were united in
a common cause against a common danger.

Raymond's crime was contumacy in not abolishing heresy. John's crime was contumacy in not accepting Langton. In both cases, the crime was against the Church. In both cases, the Church had threatened confiscation of the territory ruled by the contumacious Princes. In both cases, Philip of France was the secular power to be called upon to execute the sentence decreed by the Church.

In the Book of the Graal, Gawain bears with him to the Castle of King Fisherman the sword wherewith John the Baptist was beheaded. In real history, Fulke brought to Rome full tidings of the martyrdom of one who had heralded the advent of the new preachers. Innocent had waited for a favourable opportunity to issue the signal for the final explosion. The news that Fulke brought determined the moment. On March 10, 1208, Innocent writes to Philip and the whole temporal and spiritual hierarchy of France setting forth the story of the martyrdom, and urging immediate invasion of Raymond's dominions. 'Up, Knight of Christ! Up, most Christian Prince! . . . Hearken to the voice of the blood of the just that cries aloud to you! Gird on the shield of faith for the protection of the Church against the tyrant and the enemy! . . . Let the sword of the spirit and the sword of the flesh each come to the succour of the other ! ' The Albigensian Crusade is already on the march.

Precisely at this point a highly important piece of evidence comes into view, to which none of our historians seem to have directed their attention. The order for proclaiming the French Crusade is dated November 17, 1207, and that for promulgating the English Interdict the next day. The final letter to Philip and the French nobles proclaiming the actual commencement of the crusade is dated March 8, 1208, but there is no corresponding document in the papal archives actually proclaiming the commencement of the English Interdict. As a matter of fact, the Interdict was promulgated in England on March 23, 1208 ; and if any decisive order for its promulgation was ever issued from the papal chancery, it must have been dated at the very least a full month before, in order to allow time for the messenger to reach England, and for the Commissioners to make the necessary arrangements. It is true that even an important document of the kind might have been lost, although it is unlikely that there would be no record of its existence either in the register of papal letters or the pages of English chroniclers.

Direct evidence, however, exists, which shows clearly that the document has not been lost from the Roman archives.

Just at the time that he wrote his final injunctions to Philip to march on Languedoc, probably on the same day or the next, Innocent wrote also to the Cistercian Abbots of Persigny and du Pin. His instructions to them were to see both Philip of France and John of England personally, and to urge upon both the necessity of concluding a truce for two years in order that the crusade against Raymond and the heretics might be carried through without hindrance. The letter is one that marks its own date, because it mentions the murder of Peter of Castelnau as affording good reason for prosecuting the crusade with greater activity. Such a letter, obviously, would not be issued from the papal chancery either contemporaneously with or later than a letter giving the final order for putting the Interdict in force in John's dominions. Yet that the final order was issued before March 8, is clear from the fact that the Interdict was actually promulgated in England on March 23. The inference, then, seems clear, that the final order on which the Interdict Commissioners acted did not emanate from the Roman chancery. But if not, there is but one other source from which it can have emanated—to wit, from Arnold of Cîteaux, the recognised chief of the papal executive. It may be urged—and this is the view of Lingard and others—that in giving full powers to the Interdict Commissioners in the previous November, Innocent left it to them to decide when the Interdict should actually commence, and that the choice of March 23 was the date they fixed on their own authority without any further reference to Rome being made. This certainly is possible, but exceedingly improbable. After receiving their instructions in November, the three Bishops had had an interview with John, who had laughed at their menace, and sworn by the teeth of God to slit the noses and tear out the eyes of any traitor who should dare to publish the Interdict. They knew that their lives were in jeopardy, and, brave men as they were, they were exceedingly unlikely to proceed to the last extremity without definite orders from headquarters. At least, as men of common-sense as well as courage, they would not run the gratuitous risk of being accused of having acted precipitately. The real fact seems to me to be that Arnold deliberately forced Innocent's hand. Innocent was anxious, as his letter to the two Abbots indicates, to get matters settled in Languedoc first, and to postpone for the time any extreme measures in England. Arnold, sold body and soul for the time-being to Philip of France, and jealous beyond measure at the management of the English Interdict having been taken out of his hands and placed in those of the Bishops, was determined, if possible, to unite the Interdict and the Crusade, and carry on the war simultaneously in England and Languedoc in the interests of Philip.

This view of the case exactly coincides with the known facts. The murder of Peter of Castelnau took place January 15, 1208, when Arnold was absent from Languedoc negotiating with Philip somewhere within Philip's own dominions. The news would probably reach Arnold from S. Gilles a very few days later, as his immediate return into Languedoc would be absolutely indispensable at such a juncture. On receiving the tidings, Arnold's first business would be to seek another interview with Philip. On discussing the new situation created by the murder, it could not fail to be seen how decisively Philip's cause must be strengthened in Languedoc by that event; and Arnold, it may safely be assumed, would exhort Philip by every temporal and spiritual consideration he could urge, not to let slip so golden an opportunity of at once commencing the double campaign against Raymond of Toulouse, and Raymond's brother by marriage and by community of crime, John of England. That Philip and Arnold before parting had come to a definite understanding with regard to the policy to be pursued is certain. What that policy was may be gathered with almost equal certainty from the subsequent conduct of both.

His final negotiations with Philip would probably not detain Arnold more than forty-eight hours at most, and his next business would be to rejoin the band of preachers in the South at the earliest possible moment. Before his arrival, Fulke and Navarre were already on their way to Rome. Arnold, however, drew up and despatched what may be termed the official report of the martyrdom, which re-appears in Innocent's letters to Philip of March 8, and which, consequently, must have reached Rome some days before. If, as I believe was the case, Arnold despatched at the same time a peremptory order to the Commissioners in England to commence the Interdict, the absence from the papal registers of any order for commencing it, the actual date of the commencement, and, above all, Innocent's ignorance of the fact that any order for its commencement had been issued, are all simply and naturally explained. Nor, supposing Arnold to have issued such an order, was he guilty of any disobedience. The only offence with which he could be charged by Innocent was 'presumption' in acting *ultra vires* in a matter which might well be regarded as within his jurisdiction. 'Moses,' Arnold, was the recognised executive of 'Aaron,' Innocent. Plenary power in reference to Interdict in Languedoc had been formally conferred upon him. He had just concluded preliminary negotiations with Philip. Surely, it would be no unpardonable stretch of authority for Arnold to dictate the time for commencing the Interdict in England.

The tension between Innocent and Arnold soon reached an acuter stage. The Interdict began in England on March 23, 1208. In some cases, it seems to have begun the day before ; in others, a day or several days later ; but, on the whole, the incidence of the Curse on the Kingdom of Logres from Land's End to the Border was practically simultaneous. John's first impulse was revenge. His second was compromise. Hugh, Abbot of Beaulieu,

John's own Cistercian foundation in the New Forest, was chosen as his fittest diplomatist to plead his cause with Innocent. According to custom, the Archbishops of Canterbury received the regalia of their office from the King, and their *pallium* from the Pope. John intrusted the regalia to Hugh's charge, bidding him tell the Pope to dispose of them as he pleased The Abbot left injunctions to the brethren of Beaulieu not to obey the Interdict within the precincts of the abbey so lately founded by his royal master, and started at once for Rome. That the orders were punctually obeyed appears from the minutes of the next General Chapter of the Order held in the following September. On this occasion, all the English Abbots who had presumed 'to obey the sentence of Interdict against the immunities of the Order' were enjoined three days' penance, one on bread and water, for the offence. The three Abbots, however, of Margan, Meaux, and Beaulieu were exempted 'because they stood up for the liberty of the Order.' When the General Chapter of Cîteaux inflicts penance on the English Abbots for obeying the commands of Rome and the Commissioners appointed by Rome, it is clear that the relations between Innocent and Arnold are not precisely those that ought to exist between Moses and Aaron, or Paul and Peter.

Hugh's mission at first seemed to promise well. On May 27, Innocent writes to John. Hugh, he says, 'has told me that you are prepared to accept Stephen Langton as Archbishop, to make restitution for what you have plundered from the Church, and to allow the monks of Canterbury to return in peace. He has further placed the regalia in my hands with the message that I am to do with them what I please. When I asked the Abbot why you would not confer the regalia yourself, he said that you could not at present bring your mind to receive the Archbishop into grace with any feeling of fellowship. In consequence, after taking counsel with my brethren, I think the best way of proceeding will be for me to receive them without prejudice to your rights or mine, and deliver them to the Bishops of London, Ely, and Worcester'—the Commissioners of the Interdict—'to confer on the Archbishop on my behalf, if you really cannot make up your mind to confer them yourself. This done, and the Archbishop enthroned at Canterbury, they will then relax the Interdict; and I have written to the Archbishop himself

so to behave towards you as to deserve your
favour to the profit of the Church committed to
his care. I do, however, again most earnestly
beseech and exhort your Majesty as a personal
favour to confer the regalia yourself, as an
act more honourable alike to you and to the
Church. But however this may be, I do
most confidently commend the Archbishop
and the Church of Canterbury to God most
high ; and, through the Archbishop, do in
absolute good faith commend myself to you,
well knowing that he will show himself
worthy of your confidence and favour.'

At this time, clearly, Innocent saw no insuperable difficulty in the way of relaxing the
Interdict. It had been begun earlier than he
had intended, but he thought he already saw
a way out of the difficulty. The situation,
however, was complicated as well as difficult.
John's eldest half-brother, the Archbishop of
York, Geoffry the turbulent, had resisted one
of John's many unconstitutional exactions. In
revenge, John had laid hands on the ecclesiastical revenues of the see, and driven the Archbishop into exile. The province of York had
consequently been laid under a special interdict
of its own shortly before the wider general
interdict had been laid upon the whole kingdom.

At this juncture, therefore, the Archbishops of both provinces were excluded not only from their sees, but from the country, and John was plundering both churches in order to carry on the war against the Church. Abbot Hugh had not been instructed to say anything about the business of the northern Archbishopric. Innocent, however, had no mind to dissociate the North from the South in coming to a settlement with John. On the same day, therefore, that he wrote to John, he wrote also to the Commissioners of the Interdict in the province of York, the Bishops of London and Rochester, and the Dean of Lincoln, warning them that they were not to relax the Interdict in the province of York until the Archbishop had been restored to the see, and restitution made to the Church. If Stephen were admitted to Canterbury, the Interdict would be lifted from England, but the antecedent Interdict in the province of York would still remain in force, to be relaxed only when Geoffry should be restored to York.

These letters were written at the end of May. On June 21 an event occurred which profoundly affected the policy of Innocent, Philip, and John. This was the assassination of the Suabian Emperor, Philip, son of Frederic

Barbarossa. For a moment, Philip of France seems to have contemplated competing for the vacant throne of the Empire. If he did, no long reflection was needed to convince him that it was more expedient to defer his ambition. John still had broad lands in the South. His wealth was still supposed to be inexhaustible. He was still confident of recovering the continental provinces he had lost. Ferrand of Flanders, less powerful than John, was no less deadly a foe. Philip had sworn that Flanders should be French, and the invasion had already begun. Raymond of Toulouse was still friendly, but the crusade against the Albigenses was nothing less than a masked invasion of the South; and as soon as Raymond understood the truth, his enmity must be expected. Burgundy, Lombardy even, he might hope to win by patience, but to grasp at the Empire would be to imperil, perhaps destroy, all hope of future success.

There were three principal competitors for the Imperial Crown—Otho of Brunswick, the young Frederic of Sicily, and Henry of Brabant. Philip of France favoured the last and assisted him with funds. Both Innocent and John declared in favour of John's nephew, Otho of Brunswick. This coincidence of interest in a

matter of such vital interest to both naturally
tended for the time-being to mitigate the
asperities of the conflict on the subject of the
Interdict. Each was anxious to conciliate the
other so long at least as the election of Emperor
was still pending. Innocent flattered himself
that he could employ the occasion as a lever to
open the door for Stephen and Geoffry to take
possession of their sees. John flattered himself
that he could employ it as an instrument for
Innocent's discomfiture.

The mollifying influence of this community
of interest is perceptible throughout all the
earlier stages of the Interdict. On July 14,
letters of safe-conduct were granted by John to
Stephen's brother, Simon Langton, as well as
to the three Interdict Commissioners, to pass
freely to and fro between Dover and the Con-
tinent till September 8, and the permission was
subsequently extended to the end of the month.
In the beginning of August, Innocent writes
again to John, but his letter breathes no hint of
Interdict. Now is the time for John to come
forward with a subvention on behalf of Otho
worthy of the richest king in Christendom.
If he will only behave like a generous uncle on
the occasion, writes Innocent, John will not
only help his nephew immensely, but also

magnify himself beyond anything that it is expedient to put into black and white in a letter. In this particular matter, John was quite willing to oblige. He knew he could rely on Otho to turn traitor to Innocent at the earliest opportunity. He even sent promises of making full satisfaction for his sins against the Church. In September, letters of safe-conduct were granted by John to Stephen himself for three weeks ; but the Archbishop, doubtless for good reason, forbore to make any use of them.

Before this time, Innocent had become aware that in addition to his difficulties with John, he had to reckon with the intrigues not only of Philip of France, but of Philip's ally, Arnold of Cîteaux. On August 22, he writes again to the Interdict Commissioners. Certain ' angels of evil ' have been suggesting that he is about to relax the Interdict. He will do nothing of the kind until John has accepted his conditions and given adequate security for their fulfilment. ' This,' he writes, ' is the tenor of our mandate according to the discreet and simple under-standing thereof, clearly expressed in our former letters, and carefully explained to our dearly beloved son the Abbot of Beaulieu, the envoy of the foresaid king. Wherefore we hold it

not only an unworthy but an impious act of
any man sacrilegiously to assert or believe that
we have explained our intentions in one way to
one, and in another to another.' The 'angels
of evil' responsible for the slander are not
mentioned by name, but the chief culprit is
clearly indicated in a later passage of the same
letter : 'But you ought to know that this
hath reached our ears. After all the monks of
the Cistercian Order, in common with the
others, had begun to observe the sentence of
Interdict; within the course of a few days,
certain of them celebrated Mass on their own
authority, while others, at a considerably later
period, began to celebrate in accordance with
a mandate from the Abbot of Cîteaux, others
again still observing the Interdict. Now, as
we remember to have made answer to you in
former letters, supposing it had been allowed
from the beginning for monks to celebrate
divine service according to the tenor of their
privileges, with closed doors, without ringing
of bells, and in a low voice, it would have been
neither offensive nor disagreeable to us. But
now, if the sentence is hereby to be impaired
and the business shorn of its vigour, whatsoever
may be the grounds on which certain of the
monks have proceeded to celebrate—whether

it be on account of that clause granted them by the Apostolic See, to wit, that no letters obtained against the tenor of their apostolic privileges shall have validity as against the Cistercians unless the name of the Order be expressly mentioned therein—or whether on account of the answer that was formerly sent, which haply has reached them through somebody revealing it,—in any case, you may confidently rely on our authority in making any ordinance you may consider that the business demands, and in causing your ordinance to be firmly observed by ecclesiastical censure without appeal. Moreover, you will discreetly admonish and efficiently urge the said King to carry out without delay or demur all that the Abbot of Beaulieu promised and offered on his behalf as above expressed, seeing that, without doubt, it is as much to his practical advantage as to his safety that he should be regarded by all as having obtained the plenary grace and favour of the Apostolic See. Nor can we disguise the fact that we shall make heavy our hands against him if haply his heart shall continue so hardened that he doth not take heed to make satisfaction to God and the Church.'

To Arnold himself he writes much in the

same terms with regard to the action taken by the Commissioners, but rates him roundly for having incited the Cistercians to disobey the rescript issued by them: 'When you were consulted on the matter, you made answer to the inquirers that they could defend themselves as against the said Commissioners by interposing an appeal, unless a copy of the rescript had been actually delivered to them, or in case it should appear that the rescript had been clandestinely obtained. No doubt, according to the strict letter of the law, it was open to you to suggest a quibbling subterfuge of the kind by way of answer; but you had no right to suspect dignitaries and prelates of such high character and merit of rashly arrogating to themselves an authority we had not conferred upon them, or of maliciously wresting such authority after it had been conferred to other purposes. In this case, when it was your duty to measure other men's motives by your own, it was specially unseemly on your part to suggest a suspicion of the kind; for, if the Commissioners had stumbled on a like suspicion as against yourself, you would have been likely enough to infer that their own consciences supplied the stone.' He then formally ratifies the rescript, and commands its exact observance. The real sting of the rebuke is not revealed in the letter. In the first years of the century, the Abbey of Molême had lapsed into a state of temporal and spiritual decay. Letters had been obtained from Innocent appointing Arnold as visitor; and under his rule the Abbey had been rapidly restored to its former prosperity. Shortly before the date of Innocent's letter to Arnold, the convent had petitioned Innocent to be relieved from Arnold's annual visitation. It was surreptitiously obtained, they said, in the first instance, was now not only useless but unduly expensive, and there was good reason to fear that under pretence of visitation, Cîteaux would usurp the right of ordering their affairs in perpetuity. Innocent sent the Bishop of Troyes to inquire into the allegations and grant the petition. Arnold, he writes to the Abbot and convent, is now engaged in his duties against the heretics in Languedoc, and cannot undertake the business of visitation, even if it were expedient; and moreover, 'as you observe in your petition, it is necessary to take precautions against his turning the visitation into a pretext for usurping the regulation of the monastery in perpetuity.' He does not in so many words accuse Arnold of having obtained the letters clandestinely, but he leaves it to be clearly inferred that he did so. It was Molême from whence the first founder of Cîteaux had gone forth with his companions. The letter to the Abbot was written only a few days after that to Arnold, and the evidence of Arnold's having obtained the letters surreptitiously must have been before Innocent at the time he penned the rebuke.

With the year 1209, the Interdict in England and the Crusade in Languedoc entered on a new phase. On January 12, Innocent writes to warn John that three months after he has either received or refused to receive the present letter, sentence of anathema will be pronounced against him unless he is then prepared to fulfil all the promises he made through the Abbot of Beaulieu. Between the personal excommunication thus threatened and the actual launching of a Crusade against him there was but a single step, the declaration of deposition and the release of his subjects from their allegiance. John knew perfectly what he had to expect in case of continued contumacy. A copy of the letter to John was sent to the Commissioners with strict injunctions to them punctually to carry out the threat if John continued stubborn. In another letter of the same date he informs the Commissioners that Archbishop Stephen has petitioned that in those conventual churches which have so far strictly obeyed the Interdict, leave may be given to celebrate Mass under the usual Interdict conditions. He will not interfere himself, but leaves the matter to their discretion. A copy of the letter to John is still extant with the note in a probably contemporary hand: 'Done in the year of grace 1209, at the time the community of the faithful started on its way against the Albigensian heretics.' The coincidence of the two events, which the old scribe obviously regarded as significant, seems to have escaped the notice of later historians.

A fortnight later, February 3, another vast budget of letters issued from the papal chancery. The first was addressed to Philip urging him to appoint by royal authority some man, energetic, prudent, and faithful, to be sole captain of the host assembled for the extermination of the Provençal heretics, 'one capable of leading them that fight the battle of the Lord under God's protection and under your banner.' As a matter of history, the 'sole Captain' appointed at this time was none other than Arnold of Cîteaux himself. The next

letters are addressed to the hosts of the faithful
generally : 'Onward, ye most puissant Knights
of Christ! Onward, ye doughtiest champions
of Christian soldierhood! Aforetime, haply,
ye have fought for transitory glory—fight ye
now for glory everlasting! Ye have fought
for the body—fight ye now for the soul! Ye
have fought for the world—fight ye now for
God! Not for any earthly hire do we exhort
you to so great service to God, but for the
kingdom of God, which we do most confidently
promise shall be your reward!'

With this somewhat dithyrambic farewell,
the Crusaders may be left for the present.
Before starting as generalissimo of the armies
of God in Languedoc, Arnold did his best to
raise the devil in England. A letter of Innocent's to all the English Bishops was issued on
February 21, and records the result:—

'Whereas the monasteries of the Cistercian
Order established throughout England had
begun to observe strictly the ecclesiastical
Interdict therein generally promulgated by our
authority in the matter of the Church of
Canterbury, yet since then, as we have heard,
certain of them, under pretence of an appeal
which they are said to have interposed on the
ground of their privileges, have rashly violated

the Interdict, not only according to the terms
of their privileges, but have actually presumed
to celebrate divine service with more than
usual solemnities, with pealing of bells and
shouting of hymns, with open doors, and with
invitations to others, not Cistercians, to join in
the Communion. Albeit, therefore, we find
it hardly possible to believe that men of
religion should be guilty of such presumptu-
ous audacity, yet, since if what is asserted be
true it is impossible but that the vigour of
canonical discipline should be thereby weak-
ened, to the grievous peril of ecclesiastical
freedom, we do hereby enjoin and strictly
command every one of you most diligently to
inquire into the truth of this report, to suspend
the Abbots and Priors of such monasteries as
you shall find thus to have celebrated divine
service, and compel them to come before our
presence by ecclesiastical censure without
contradiction or the interposition of any
appeal, there to make satisfaction for so gross
a contempt. The monasteries themselves also
you shall compel by like censure inviolably to
observe the Interdict aforesaid according to the
ordinance of our venerable brethren the Bishop
of London and his co-executors, any privilege
to the contrary notwithstanding, inasmuch as

no privilege can prevail against the mandate of the Apostolic authority, privileges of the kind being always granted with a reservation of its rights.'

Writing to Arnold himself, Innocent throws upon him the entire responsibility for the state of things described, and characterises his conduct as unkind and unworthy. After rehearsing his letter to the Bishops, Innocent proceeds: ' We feel the indignity thus offered by the Cistercian Order all the harder to bear because both the Apostolic See and ourselves have so little deserved that our grace should be repaid by injury, and the honour we have done the Order by contempt. Indeed, were it not that the earnest sincerity of the love we bear towards you and other religious of the Order restrains the natural impulse of our mind, we should have taken care to punish those guilty of a temerity of this kind with a heavier chastisement. . . . We are hurt and grieved that so gross a contempt should be, as it seems to be, the result of your exhortations. It is true, as you observe in your last letter to us, and we in ours to you, that when we discussed the matter familiarly in private, we found it impossible to come to any agreement. You will nevertheless please to accept what is stated

above on the understanding that you are to
prevent others of your Order from committing
a like offence, lest haply a like punishment or
one heavier than that now inflicted should
chance to befall them ; for, assuredly, in case
you attempt to act otherwise, which we do not
believe you will, we will punish both head and
members with condign chastisement according
to the guilt of head or members.

This is 'faithful dealing.' Arnold and the
Order had no choice but to submit. Arnold's
time and energies were just now absorbed in
fulfilling the duties of Military Commander-
in-Chief, and the Order could not hope in his
absence to continue the struggle against Innocent in England. The Cistercian Abbots, however, pleaded their apology and their cause
with Innocent in the shape of a petition to
which he replied on March 6. In this petition
they set forth their case and defended the
action they had taken on four principal grounds.
The first prayer is that their privilege to celebrate in time of Interdict may be allowed.
The privilege, they assert, has been approved
by ancient custom never hitherto violated, and
they have done nothing to deserve its violation
now. To this Innocent answers that he would
have been pleased if the Commissioners had

seen their way to allowing the privilege ; but
as they were invested with Apostolic authority,
he was not in a position to interfere. The privilege was granted originally 'without prejudice'
to the Apostolic authority, which consequently
was free to override it whenever expedient.
The privilege itself and the custom founded on
the privilege remained intact. In this particular case, the Apostolic authority, as it had a
perfect right to do, had set the privilege aside.
It was perhaps to be regretted that the Commissioners took the view they did, but the
decision rested with them, not with either
Rome or Cîteaux. They had decided, and
their decision must at all costs be upheld.
The words Innocent employs are remarkable :
'You seem to have remembered to ask when
it was too late. You yourselves began by
observing the Interdict without paying heed
either to the privilege or the custom, and now
you come running back to us with your
belated petitions.'

Quite apart from technical and legal considerations, however, Innocent has good grounds
for refusing the petition. If it were granted,
would not the king with whom we are wrest-
ling, feeling our grip slacken, gather strength
from our weakness? Would not the secular

clergy and the monks of other Orders be sorely scandalised ? ' They are always more or less jealous of your Order, because you receive the tithes that they have to pay, and, just now, when they are deriving some small comfort from having you as companions in misfortune, would they not feel doubly sore were they to see you resuming the celebration of divine service while they are still condemned to keep silence ? ' They are all eager to abolish the invidious distinctions that you enjoy over themselves. Surely this is not the time to emphasise and exaggerate them ? Again, think of the slight that would be cast upon the Commissioners. They have dared the king's wrath —they have suffered exile—they are ready to suffer to the death. Would it not be intolerably mean to rebuke them for their good deeds ?

You state in your petition that the breach of the custom of celebration may result in the dissolution of your Order. The danger, if danger it be, is comparatively small. The struggle is for the liberty of the Church universal, and it is obviously better that a part should suffer than that the whole should be destroyed. Innocent's consolatory style is delightful. There is no fear, he adds, of your not being otherwise strong enough by God's help to preserve yourselves from dissolution of any such kind.

The last point in your petition is that the wrath of God, in whose hands is the heart of the king, will be sooner appeased by your celebrating the sacrifice of the Holy Eucharist. There is no harm in holding a pious opinion of the kind. It is to be hoped, however, that if you bear with patience the unmerited punishment that has befallen you, the Spirit which ever pleadeth for you with groanings unspeakable will speedily obtain a happy ending from Him who hath redeemed us by suffering punishment undeserved. Wherefore, most beloved sons, since this business is even now as it were at an end, we pray and beseech you that you interfere not to disturb it, but rather pray God that He so soften the doer of the sin as that he may pardon them that inflict the punishment, in the certain hope that a worthy recompense for unworthy punishment is reserved for you not only by God, but by ourselves.

On the same day that he sent this epistle in answer to the Cistercian petition, Innocent wrote also to the Interdict executors, asking them, if it could be done without grave scandal or too great a breach of ecclesiastical

discipline, kindly to relax the severity of the
Interdict so far as to allow the Cistercians the
exercise of their customary privilege. 'It would
have been acceptable to us,' he writes, 'if the
rigour of the Interdict had been modified from
the beginning in accordance with their privilege.' He had reason to regard Arnold as a
traitor and an enemy; but Arnold's exuberant
energy would be well employed in Languedoc,
and Innocent sincerely loved the Order whose
services he found so indispensable.

There is no need at present to follow either
Crusade or Interdict further. King Fisherman
himself has revealed the nature of the question
left unasked: 'You seem to have remembered
to ask when it was too late. You yourselves
began by observing the Interdict without
paying heed to the privilege or the custom, and
now you come running back to us with your
belated petitions.' So writes King Fisherman
to the Cistercian brotherhood. The echoes of
the words reverberate through all the winding
alleys of all romances of the Graal. In those
familiar discussions with the King of the Lower
Folk to which he refers, he might well have
stated his case a little more fully. 'Years
ago, when Dominic was here in Rome, he
petitioned me to grant him a commission to

come to your assistance in Languedoc. He was anxious that his new scheme of preaching should have a fair trial, and was careful to stipulate that all the privileges enjoyed by your Cistercians *in partibus hæreticorum* should be extended to the new preachers. But he breathed no word about privileges for you or himself *in partibus fidelium*. Fulke of Marseilles, too, our dear brother of Toulouse, was here but a day or two since to bring tidings of our Legate Peter's blessed martyrdom and to ask me to appoint new Legates to take the place of Peter and Ralph of Fontfroid. Here is your Crusade ready to start; and in discussing the requisite provision to be made during the campaign, the question of your privileges during Interdict were carefully considered. We talked, too, long and earnestly about the Interdict in England, but still not a word did he say about your privilege at such a time. If either one or the other had remembered to make inquiry, you know how gladly I would have granted any boon in reason to my dear Cistercian brethren. But it is now too late to appeal to me. My honour is pledged to the Commissioners to uphold their decision on every point connected with the Interdict. I would make any sacrifice but that of honour and religion to alleviate as far as possible the curse I have reluctantly found it necessary to inflict on the land of Logres, but what you now ask is already beyond my power. You speak too late ! ' Substitute the name of Perceval for that of Dominic, and Gawain for Fulke of Marseilles, and we have here the groundwork of the story of the Graal. There is, indeed, in Innocent's letters but little trace of the ' languishment' into which King Fisherman falls on account of the unasked question, but the metaphor aptly expresses the meaning of the Cistercian romancer. The ' languishment' that overtakes the Head of the Church is simply his way of indicating the unrelieved spiritual desolation that fell with the Interdict on the Church in England.

I do not propose to follow any further the story either of the Crusade or the Interdict. My object here is simply to throw light on the origin and motive of the story of the Graal, not to analyse its various episodes or to trace their correspondence with actual events recorded in history. If my suggestions as to the time and place in which the drama is supposed to be enacted, and my identifications of some of the principal *dramatis personæ*, are correct, the reading of the play itself will at least present far fewer difficulties to the student. The lock of the old legend is rusty, and a considerable accumulation of old oil, dirt, and cobwebs has gathered among the springs and wards ; but if the key is the true key, it will still turn the bolt and allow free entrance into the haunted chamber to examine the furniture and tapestries at leisure.

It may be useful here to put together the parallels already traced between the personages and events that figure in the romance of the Graal and the personages and events that find a place in the history of the first decade of the thirteenth century. In the romance : King Fisherman dwells in a castle where blood falls drop by drop into a holy vessel called the Graal. The contents of the Graal are served to the inmates of the castle and to any guests that have approved themselves worthy to partake of them. The food is abundant for all, and the savour is sweeter than that of any earthly meat. King Fisherman has a sister, Yglais, and two brothers, the King of Castle Mortal and the King of the Lower Folk. Once upon a time Perceval, the son of Yglais by her husband Alain li Gros, comes as a guest to the Castle of the Graal. To him, as to the household of the castle, the contents of the Graal are served, but he forbears to ask what the contents may be, or to whom they are of right administered. In consequence of the omission, a grievous misfortune falls upon England, all Christendom is plunged into a state of civil war, and King Fisherman is afflicted with a fatal 'languishment.' At a later period, Gawain also arrives at the castle, bearing with him the sword wherewith John the Baptist was beheaded. The Graal is revealed to him, but, like Perceval, he forgets to ask the question, although he has been repeatedly admonished to do so, by King Fisherman himself among others, who in consequence of the omission falls into even more grievous 'languishment' than ever.

In actual history : Dominic arrives at Rome in order to confer with Pope Innocent III. at a time when Innocent and almost the whole Catholic world had already approved of the doctrine of Transubstantiation, but when the doctrine had not yet been declared *de Fide*. Dominic is a true son of Yglais, the Church, and spiritually of the *Doctor Universalis*, Alanus, or Alain li Gros, whose arguments against the Waldenses and Albigenses he is anxious to employ in preaching to the heretics themselves. At this time, Innocent's Cistercian legates in Languedoc had already been granted absolute power in the matter of Interdict. A bishop or archbishop might lay this or that church or parish, or even his whole diocese or province, under Interdict ; but the Legates could, if so minded, not only disregard it but abrogate it, and lay a stronger interdict of their own on the *puisné* prelate. Their old privilege entitled the Cistercians to celebrate mass during Interdict privately and under certain conditions. Their privilege in Languedoc entitled them to celebrate it publicly and without conditions. Innocent conferred on Dominic the right to share in all the Cistercian privileges in Languedoc. He could not in the circumstances do otherwise, as Dominic's commission was to preach in co-operation with the Cistercian Legates. Dominic, intent on his own work, never thought of the question of privilege to celebrate mass during Interdict elsewhere than in his own special field of labour. His neglect to do so was unobserved until some few years later, when England was laid under Interdict. It was then felt that if he had only broached the question at the time of his visit, Innocent would, as he himself bears witness, have been glad to confirm at least all the ordinary privileges of the Cistercians in times of Interdict, not only in Languedoc, but throughout Christen-

dom. Had Dominic thought of the matter,
the severity of the Interdict would have been
mitigated to a great extent. Not only the
Cistercians but the friends of the Cistercians
would have still been able to partake of the
Holy Eucharist, the denial of which to all was
the heaviest part of the sentence.

Just on the eve of the Crusade and Interdict,
Fulke of Marseilles also visited Rome, bearing
full tidings of the death of Peter of Castelnau.
At such a moment, it might well have been
expected that the question of privilege during
Interdict in England would have been raised.
Fulke, however, at the time was wholly preoc-
cupied by the Albigensian Crusade, and English
affairs had less interest for him than for either
Innocent or Arnold of Cîteaux. The question
was not asked, in spite of hints from various
quarters, and, quite possibly, from Innocent
himself. The Interdict was put into force in
England in all its rigour only a few days later,
and the Cistercians no less than others were
forbidden to celebrate Mass. All but three
monasteries at first obeyed the ordinance. A
little later, by the advice of Arnold of Cîteaux,
many of them began to celebrate in accordance
with their old privilege, some in accordance
with the larger privileges enjoyed in Languedoc.

Innocent commanded instant obedience and the punishment of the principal offenders. The Cistercians thereupon 'came running back to him with their belated petitions' to be allowed to celebrate Mass, but were met with the response that they had remembered to ask the boon too late.

This is not a mere similarity, it is identity. The persons and things are the same both in the Romance and in the History. Innocent describes himself as called to the office of Fisherman. King Fisherman is the guardian of the Graal. He has the power of withholding the celebration of the Mass by Interdict or granting it by privilege. Dominic is in simple fact the spiritual son of the Church and of Alanus. The Interdict is as a matter of history the sorest spiritual mischance that had ever befallen Great Britain. It is on authentic record that the failure to obtain any settlement of the question as to the celebration of the Holy Sacrament during Interdict did lead to serious strife in the Church, and very materially aggravated the hardships of the curse that fell upon the kingdom of Logres. Innocent himself bears witness that he would have been only too pleased to grant a favourable answer had the question been raised in time. It

is no ordinary allegory. The story - teller
calls Innocent King Fisherman and Dominic
Perceval, just as he would call a fox Reynard,
or a bear Bruin. John Bunyan's ' Giant Pope '
is a personification of the Papacy as an insti-
tution. The Romancer's King Fisherman is
the Pope himself, who happens just now to be
Innocent III.

Coincidences of the kind I have pointed out
do not happen fortuitously. There are far too
many of them all pointing at once in the same
direction for them to be the result of accident.
The central idea of the story, the conception
of illimitable warfare and desolation, of smitten
kings, and kingdoms groaning under the curse
of Heaven as the disastrous consequences of
a young knight inadvertently omitting to
ask a question which might well seem to be
impertinent at the court of a highly devout
King who happened to be a Fisherman, is on
the face of it grotesque, unintelligible, in-
credible, incoherent as lunacy itself. It is
an idea that no poet or romancer would have
hit on *à priori* as his theme. It could not have
occurred to him before the event had happened
in reality. The event itself, too, never
happened, never could happen, but once. It
is absolutely unique in the world's history.

Consequences of not asking a question at the right time have perhaps been even more disastrous. No other heavy curse ever fell on the kingdom of Logres because of a question unasked at the court of a King who was also a Fisherman. No other event could possibly have suggested the Romance as it stands. No figment so wild was ever so true to actual fact. Had no other interpretation ever been placed upon the legend, I venture to believe that no other would ever have obtained even a temporary acceptance from those to whom the history of the time is as familiar as the legend of the Graal itself.

IV

ELUCIDATION

Car vous n'oistes ains parler
Veraiement ne raconter;
Et si fu grans noise et grans bruis
Coment et por coi fu destruis
De Logres li rices pais ;
Moult en sot-an parler jadis.

(ÉLUCIDATION DE L'HYSTOIRE DU
GRAAL, 23.)

So far, attention has been called only to the
central idea as set forth in the 'High History
of the Holy Graal.' There are, however, a
number of other versions of the story, and it
may, perhaps, be reasonably surmised that the
interpretation of some of these is not to be
found in the events to which I have referred.
This, however, is not the case. Each version
has its own special and peculiar key, but the
master-key unlocks them all. In all, King
Fisherman, by whatever name he may be
called, is the Pope. In all which make mention
of the curse that fell upon Logres, 'the event

referred to is the Interdict. In all, Perceval is none other than Dominic. Innumerable accretions, variations, transpositions, substitutions, superfluities, are to be found, but these elements remain constant. They underlie alike the versions redacted by Malory and the *Parzival* of Wolfram von Eschenbach.

For the purposes of this introduction, it will be enough to examine one fragment only of another version of the story, chosen from the immense mass of material still extant, because it has already for more than three centuries and a half been recognised as an ' Elucidation ' of the story of the Graal. The original from which I translate is the beginning of the second volume of *Perceval le Gallois*, edited by M. Ch. Potvin for the *Société des Bibliophiles Belges*, Mons, 1866. M. Potvin prints it as part of the work by Chrestien de Troyes, to whose poem on the history of Perceval it serves as an introduction. The question as to its true authorship need not be here discussed. It is agreed on all hands that it is part of a very early version of the story, and, as such, it was with the rest of the poem turned into prose and published in Paris in 1530, with the side-note, '*Élucidation de l'hystoire du Graal.*' The date I assign to the lines here rendered in

literal prose is somewhere between 1220 and
1225 :—

'By way of a noble commencement thereof,
here worshipfully beginneth a Romance of the
most delightsome story that may be, to wit,
the story of the Graal, the secret whereof may
no man tell in prose nor rhyme, for such a
thing might the story turn out to be before it
were all told that every man might be grieved
thereof albeit he had in nowise misdone.
Wherefore it is that the wise man leaveth it
aside and doth simply pass on beyond, for, and
Master Blihis lie not, the secret should no man
tell.

'Now listen to me, all ye my friends, and ye
shall hear me set forth the story that shall be
right sweet to hearken unto, for therein shall
be the seven Wardens that hold governance
throughout the whole world, and all the good
stories that any hath told according as the
writing shall set them forth ; what manner
folk the seven Wardens should be, and how
they took unto them a chief, and whom they
took, for never aforetime have ye heard tell
the story truly set forth, and how great noise
was there and great outcry, and how and for
what cause was destroyed the rich country of
Logres whereof was much talk in days of yore.

' The kingdom turned to loss, the land was dead and desert in suchwise as that it was scarce worth a couple of hazel-nuts. For they lost the voices of the wells and the damsels that were therein. For no less thing was the service they rendered than this, that scarce any wandered by the way, whether it were at eventide or morning, but that as for drink and victual he would go so far out of his way as to find one of the wells, and then nought could he ask for of fair victual such as pleased him but incontinent he should have it all so long as he had asked in reason. For straightway, I wis, forth of the well issued a damsel—none fairer need he ask—bearing in her hand a cup of gold with larded meats, pasties, and bread, while another damsel bore a white napkin and a dish of gold or silver wherein was the mess which he that had come for the mess had asked for. Right fair welcome found he at the well, and if so it were that his mess did not please him, divers other they brought him all made to his wish with great cheer and great plenty. The damsels with one accord served fair and joyously all wayfarers by the roads that came to the wells for victual.

' King Amangons, that was evil and craven-hearted, was the first to break the custom, for

thereafter did many others the same according
to the ensample they took of the King whose
duty it was to protect the damsels and to
maintain and guard them within his peace.
One of the damsels did he enforce, and to her
sore sorrow did away her maidenhead, and
carried off from her the cup of gold that he
took along with him, and afterward did make
him every day be served thereof. Well
deserved he to come to mishap thereby. For
thenceforth never did the damsel serve any
more nor issue forth of that well for no man
that might come thither to ask for victual.
And all the other damsels only served in such
sort as that none should see them.

'The other vassals that held of the King's
honour, when they beheld this of their Lord that
he enforced the damsels wheresoever he found
them comeliest, did all in like manner enforce
them and carried off the cups of gold in suchwise that thereafter did no damsel issue forth
of the wells nor none did service. This wot
ye well, my Lords, that on this wise did the
land turn to its downfall, and an evil end
withal did the King make and all the others
after him that had wrought the damsels sore
annoy. In such sort was the kingdom laid
waste that thenceforth was no tree leafy.

The meadows and the flowers were dried up
and the waters were shrunken, nor as then
might no man find the Court of the Rich
Fisherman that wont to make in the land a
glittering glory of gold and silver, of ermines
and minever, of rich palls of sendal, of meats
and of stuffs, of falcons gentle and merlins
and tercels and sparrow-hawks and falcons
peregrine.

'Then, when the Court was found, throughout the country was so great plenty of all
manner riches such as I have named that I
warrant you all men marvelled thereat both
rich and poor. Thenceforward, as before it
had lost every whit, so now in the kingdom
of Logres was all the richesse in the world.

'The Peers of the Table Round came in the
time of King Arthur. So good as they were
none ever seen. Knights were they so good,
so worshipful, so strong, so proud, so puissant,
and so hardy, that when they had heard the story
of the adventures, they were fain incontinent
to recover the wells. All with one accord
sware an oath to protect the damsels that had
been put out of them and the cups that had
been carried away, and to destroy root and
branch the kindred of them that had wrought
them harm. For these dwelt so nigh the wells

that the damsels came not forth; and if it were
that they could catch any of them, her made
they be slain by the sword or hanged. Alms
made they and prayer to God that He would
recover back the wells in such stablishment as
they were aforetime, and that for His honour
He would do them the service they asked of
Him. Before they bethought them of asking
so much, they could find nought. Never a
voice could they hear from the wells, nor would
no damsel issue therefrom.

'But thereafter such adventure found they
that they did very mightily marvel thereat.
For in the forest found they damsels—fairer
none would you ask—with whom were knights
right well armed upon their destriers that
protected the damsels. Together fought they
against them that would fain have carried them
off. Many a knight did they make die, for the
damsels, I wis, had many a battle in the land.
King Arthur thereby lost many a good knight
without recovery, and many a good one did he
gain thereby, as the story will tell you.

'The Knight first conquered had to name
Blihos Bliheris, and him did Messire Gauwains
overcome through the great prowess whereof
he is fulfilled. Him sent he to yield himself
up to King Arthur; whereupon he mounted

his horse as he that hath no mind to tarry; and
when he came to the Court did yield himself
up, albeit never was he there known of the
King, nor none did he know. But right good
stories he knew, such as that none could ever
be aweary of hearkening to his words. They
of the Court asked him of the damsels that
rode by the forest albeit it were not yet
summer, and good right had they so to ask
and demand answer. And he knew how to
tell them as much so that right willingly gave
they ear to him, and many a night together
were the damsels and the knights fain to
hearken to him and seek him out.

'He saith to them : "Much marvel have ye
of the damsels that ye see go among these
great forests, and never make ye an end of
asking in what country we are born. I will
tell ye the truth hereof. All we are born of
the damsels, and never in the world were
fairer, whom King Amangons did enforce.
Never on any day of the world shall those
wrongs be amended. The Peers of the Table
Round of their courtesy and honour, of their
prowess and valiance, are fain by force to
recover the wells whereof these be the squires
and knights and nobles. I will tell you the
sum of the matter. These all shall journey

in common, and the damsels in likewise that
wander at large through this country by forest
and field behoveth it thus to fare until such
time as God shall give them to find the Court
from whence shall come the joy whereby the
land shall again be made bright. To them
that shall seek the Court, shall befall adventures
such as were never found nor told of in this
land afore." Much to their liking was this that
he said and sung unto them, and right well
were they pleased.

'Thereafter was no great delay or ever the
good knights of the Court held a great parliament whereunto each made ready to repair
straightway. Right stoutly then sought they
the Court of the Rich Fisherman that could
much of nigromancy, insomuch that a hundred
times changed he his semblance in such sort
that whoso should have seen him in one guise
should not know him again when he showed
him as another man after another guess fashion.

'Messire Gauwains found the Court what
time Arthur was King, and sojourned thereat
in very sooth. That shall be well recounted
before you, and the joy that he had there,
whereof all the kingdom was the better. But
afore him, the first to find it was a young
knight that was right little of age, albeit none

more hardy of courage was not to be found in all the world. Then came to the Table Round the young man of whom I tell you that in prowess did overpass all that ever were or now are throughout all the countries of the world. Of no account was he held at first, yet afterwards was his accoutrement right noble, and so thoroughly did he search out amidst the land them that went about to conquer it, that he found the Court. This is the sooth, and many of ye know it. Perceval li Galois was he. He asked whereof the Graal served, but demanded not as to the Lance, when he saw it, wherefore it should bleed, nor of the Sword whereof the one-half was taken away and the other lay in the bier over one dead after the manner of a great swooning. But I tell you of a certainty that he made inquisition as to what was the treasure that was in the hall and the rich cross of silver that came foremost of all.

'By the space of three hours three times a day was therein lamentation so sore that no man, were he never so hardy, but and if he should hear it he should be stricken with fear. Then did they hang four censers at four rich candlesticks that were at the horns of the bier. When they had done the service, straightway the cries continued again, and every man evanished away. The hall that was great and wide remained void and astonied, and the stream of blood ran from the vessel where was the Lance through the rich channel of silver.

'Then forthwith was the palace filled of the folk and the knights. Then was the fairest victual of all the world made ready. Then issued forth in all his apparel the King that was unknown. From a chamber came he forth robed. In right noble attire he came, insomuch as that none could declare the robe nor the apparelling so overpassing rich was it, and on his finger had he a ring exceeding good, and his arms had he straitly folded, and upon his head a circle of gold whereof the stones are worth a treasure, and therewithal a full seemly buckle and girdle. Never so comely man on live could no man find. Right little might any surmise that this was he whom he had seen that day attired as a fisherman.

'So soon as the King was seated, then might you see all the knights seated at the other high tables. Then full swiftly was the bread set on and the wine placed in presence in great cups of gold and silver. Thereafter might ye see the Graal without servitor and without seneschal come through the door of a chamber and serve right worshipfully in rich dishes of gold that were worth a great treasure. The first mess did it set before the King, and then did it serve all the others round about, and nought less was it than a miracle of the messes that it brought them and the victual that it gave them. And then came the great miracle of all, whereunto is none other to be compared.

'Natheless hereof will you never hear me speak, for Percevaus ought to tell it hereafter in the midst of the story, seeing that great churlishness is it and great shame to rehearse a good story piecemeal otherwise than as of right it ought to go. When the Good Knight shall come that found the Court as three times, then shall you hear me recount point to point without feigning ought the truth as concerning the wells, whereunto they served, whereof these were the knights; and of the Graal wherefore it served, and all the manner of the Lance that bled will I tell you, and wherefore the sword was on the bier. All will I tell you in suchwise as that nought will I leave out, the lamentation, the evanishment, all will I tell such folk as shall hear me speak, in such sort as that they shall know thereafter how this work ought of right to go.

'My lords, a proven sooth it is that seven times was the Court found in the seven Cloaks of the story. But as yet ye know not what this may signify. You must understand, then, that the seven Cloaks are in truth the seven Wardens. Each of these Wardens in his turn will tell you how he found the Court, and beforehand ought it not to be told. Now behoveth me in this writing to name all the seven Wardens, for none would I fain overpass. Wherefore ought I rather to name them clearly and speak of them in the order wherein they are to be set forth.

'The seventh Branch, which is the most pleasant. This is concerning the Lance wherewith Longis smote in the side the King of holy majesty, and the sixth, without fail, of the great content of the travail. In the fifth, I shall recount ye the wrath and the loss of Huden. The story of Heaven is the fourth, for no craven was he, the knight Mors del Calan that came first to Glomorgan. The next is the third, of the warrior of whom Castrars had the great affright. Pecorins the son of Amangons carried always the scar in his forehead. Now have I named the third to you. The second is not done into verse according to the witness of good story-tellers. It would be the story of the great sorrows, how Lanselos dou Lac was there where he lost his virtue.

And afterward comes the last. Forasmuch as
I have undertaken the task, behoveth me tell it,
and you shall hear me begin without delay.
It is the adventure of the Shield, never was a
better.

'These be the seven natural stories whereof
all do move of the Graal. Such joy did this
adventure bring about, that thereupon did
the people repeople the land after the great
destruction. In very truth it was this finding
of the Court and the Graal whereby the realm
was repeopled, in suchwise that the waters
which ran not, and the fountains which flowed
not, for that they had been dried up, ran forth
amidst the meadows. Then were the fields
green and bountiful, and the woods clad in
leaves the day that the Court was found.
Throughout the country were the forests so
great and thick, so fair and fresh, that every
wayfarer journeying through the land did
marvel thereat.

'Then came back a folk full of right sore
despiteousness, they, to wit, that had come
forth of the wells but were not cooks. These
made castles and cities and burghs and strong-
holds, and made for the damsels the rich
Castle of Maidens. The Bridge Perilous
made they also, and the great Castle Orguel-

lous. For noblesse, moreover, and for lordship made they an Order of the Peers of the Rich Meinie, through great pride was it begun as against the Table Round. Well was it known of all the world that each of them had his mistress therein, and right little fair life did they lead. Three hundred and threescore and six were they that did maintain the castle, and each of these had a score knights, whereof he was lord; to the number, I ween I mistake not, were they of seven thousand six hundred and fourscore and six. But wot ye well, that all for nought did these make a stir in the world, for never a one may any longer be found therein. They rode through the land and made war upon King Arthur, and the good knights of the Court went forth to make assay of them, and wot ye well that when they caught one they loosed not their hold till they had slain him.

'King Arthur was fain to go and throw down the castle and destroy it, but all they that then did hate him did right at this very point assail him and deliver battle in such sort, that no need had he to go seek it for the nonce. So great were the wars as at this time, that they lasted a good four year, as the story telleth us.

' He also that did make the book, and so I tell ye one by one, He willeth that ye show to each man as concerning the Graal whereunto it served, for the services it wrought should be shown of a good Master, lest the good things that it serveth be not known but hidden, for freely will He teach it unto all people, even as ye have heard.

' This King Arthur of whom I speak held war against the folk of his land four years. But all this draweth he to an end, so that no man nor neighbour was there that did not his will therein, either, ye wot, of force or of good-will. This was proven truth. But wot ye moreover this, that was spoken to their shame and to the honour of the King, as most of ye know, that on the very day the Court and the Rich Meinie were set free, they went a-hunt-ing in the forest, and they that would fain go a-hawking followed the good rivers. This is how folk be of manner. Some will only have to do with disport, and others with how they shall apparel them. Nought did they but make merry the winter through until the summer.'

I have given this *Élucidation* in full, because it is not easily accessible, and is, I believe, the only fragment extant of contemporary exegesis on the story of the Graal. By far the greater part of it, however, refers directly to the identity of King Fisherman with the Pope, and of the curse that fell on the kingdom of Logres with the English Interdict. The metaphors of the 'Elucidation' are easily convertible into plain English ; and if it is lamentable to be obliged to substitute historic prose for the poetry of romance, the process at least vindicates the character of the Damsels of the Wells, somewhat unjustly compromised by the metaphorical exigencies of the case. For who are the Damsels, and what are the Wells ? The immediate cause of the 'Great Destruction,' we are told, was the violation of one of the Damsels by King Amangons, and all are in some way closely connected with the Court of King Fisherman. While the Court remains in the land, their voices are heard from the Wells, and their hospitality is freely offered to all comers. When the Court is withdrawn, they cease to serve at the Wells, and their voices are no more heard. Many of them are driven out to wander in the forest, not a few are killed outright, and the rest remain close hidden in the recesses of the Wells. When the Court is restored, the wanderers also are restored, and the Wells are served as before. Surely we need be at no loss to recognise the Wells as the churches of the land, and the Damsels with their golden cups as the benefices thereunto belonging? In very truth the churches were wells in more than one sense. William of Newbury writes of Fountains Abbey : ' The place is called " Fountains," where, then and thereafter, as it were from the fountains of the Saviour so many have drunk of the waters springing up into everlasting life.' In every church, too, was the baptismal font, the well of water sanctified to the mystical washing away of sins. In this case, at least, the metaphor verges closely on the synonym.

Nor is the identity of the Damsels harder to detect. The headings to the chapters in the Authorised Version of the 'Song of Songs, which is Solomon's' may be regarded as indicating how generally the Church has been regarded as the Bride of Christ. This primary spiritual wedlock was not less universally held to be symbolised in the relation subsisting between any spiritual cure and the ecclesiastic who held it. The ceremony of conferring a benefice—especially in those cases where it was accompanied by the delivery of a staff and ring—was always recognised as in a certain sense a solemnisation of matrimony. The

Bishop was the husband of his bishopric, the parish priest of his benefice or cure. From this point of view, the whole country was partitioned out among the spiritual wives of the clergy, while the lands belonging to the various ecclesiastical foundations were specially regarded as *sponsalia* or marriage dowries. King Fisherman himself comments on his own marriage to the Church. 'A marvellous thing is it,' writes Innocent, 'that I who have vowed celibacy, have nevertheless contracted wedlock. But this wedlock hindereth not celibacy, nor doth the fruitfulness of the wife take away the chastity of her maidenhood.' An ecclesiastical romancer, writing of a time when most of the Bishops were in exile, and a number of Abbots and beneficed clergy robbed of their revenues and ousted from their charges, would naturally picture the stricken churches as forlorn damsels wandering by fell and forest. Those, moreover, who wrought and fought to restore the Damsels to the Wells, could hardly figure otherwise, if the metaphor were to be maintained, than as the chivalrous knights who came to the succour and protection of the Damsels. It is a sore shock to the imagination to discover that the Damsels of the Wells, among the fairest creations of mediæval

romance, represent, after all, only an over-
strained metaphor of church and glebe and
parish and diocese and ecclesiastical revenue.
But this ruthless 'elucidator' really leaves no
room to doubt his meaning.   His 'golden
cups' are the incomes of the clergy, and he
means us to understand it clearly.   Quite
incidentally, however, his prosaic elucidation
certainly solves two considerable difficulties.
He satisfactorily accounts for the abnormal
number of forlorn damsels that haunted the
forests 'in the days of King Arthur,' and effectually clears their character, even when he
imputes to them conduct that transgresses the
limits even of mediæval 'propriety.'

The services the Damsels rendered freely to
all wayfarers are no metaphor.   That every
wanderer might actually claim 'bit and sup'
at the doors of many monasteries and other
religious foundations was a happy accident due
to the kindly provision of some pious founder,
patron, or brother.   That all who would and
could might hear Mass and partake of the Holy
Sacrament at the churches was a franchise of
Christendom, the privilege and birthright of
every child of Christ and Holy Church.   At a
time when the churches and religious houses
were practically the schools and school boards,

the lecture-rooms and places of public meeting, the hotels and theatres of our forefathers, no less than sanctuaries of worship, the phrases employed by the romancer to describe the blessings conferred by the Damsels of the Wells are hardly exaggerated.

A monastic writer of romance, especially a Cistercian, could not but be familiar with the figure of speech which converted religious foundations into damsels. Of one mother-monastery, for instance, we read that her three 'eldest daughters' have power over their mother in the way of visitation and correction, and may, on good cause shown, depose her Prior and elect another. A letter of Innocent III. bids the Abbot of Pontigny receive the Church of S. Martin as his 'special daughter.' Cîteaux itself had four such 'special daughters,' of whom Clairvaux is the best known. The four collegiate churches of Paris are ' daughters ' of the Cathedral Church, as is also the case at Autun and elsewhere. Sometimes the metaphor reads even more grotesquely in monastic annals than in the romance, as when the Abbot of Bonfont is solemnly sentenced by the General Chapter of Cîteaux to do penance ' for not having visited his daughter this year ' (1201), or another Abbot (1207) for having taken money 'what time he visited his daughters,' or a third because he was wont 'to visit his daughter by his monks instead of personally' (1210). We still talk of 'Mother Church' and a mother-church, but the ideas connected with the words are parochial, national, or Catholic. In the thirteenth century, every church in the land, mother, daughter, sister, or bride, was still a 'damsel,' not merely in the imagination of romancers, but in the ecclesiastical common parlance of the time. Well-nigh seven centuries have passed since the old poet saw the Damsels of the Wells riding homeless through the forests 'in the days of King Arthur,' but the ages have spared their beauty and their youth. Very fair are they still in the realm of Logres, and loud and sweet as ever are their voices to-day, voices of counsel and comfort, of prayer and praise and thanksgiving; voices, too, of other kinds that speak without words in the sound of bells and the music of organs—many voices and various, yet ever and again uniting in the burden: 'Come ye to the wells, whosoever will, and take freely of the water of life!'

But if the churches of the land be the Damsels of the Wells, who is Amangons, the King that was evil and craven-hearted? He is

not far to seek. Matthew Paris speaks of him
in much the same terms, as does almost every
other chronicler of his own or of after-time,
and with one accord they all bluntly call him
King John. The damsel he enforces is none
other than the Church of Canterbury, and the
golden cup of which he plunders her the
revenues of the see, 'whereof he did afterward
make him every day be served.' The desolat-
ing vengeance that falls upon the country in
consequence of the King's sin is the great
English Interdict. King Fisherman is, of
course, Innocent III., and his Court the entire
hierarchy of the Church in England. The
Peers of the Table Round are the allied leaders
of the twin Crusades against Raymond of
Toulouse and John of England. Perceval
again is Dominic, and Gawain Fulke of Marseilles. Other identifications, such as that of
Pecorins, son of Amangons, with Henry III., the
son of John, are obvious. Others, such as that
of Blihos Bliheris, may perhaps be conjectured.
Others, such as that of Huden, are probably
lost beyond recovery.

In order to avoid unnecessary complication,
I refrain from any comment on the personages
and events referred to in the 'Elucidation' not
connected with the central plot of the 'High

History.' Those, however, who care to search
the records of the time will find no insuperable
difficulties in the way of obtaining satisfactory
information as to the rich Castle of Maidens,
the Bridge Perilous, the great Castle Orguel-
lous, and the Order of the Peers of the Rich
Meinie. All are historic, albeit they find no
place in any of our so-called 'Histories of
England,' and their identification will be found
to be simply an extension of the identifications
here suggested to men and matters outside my
present purview. Here it will be sufficient to
show how vividly the elucidator elucidates and
confirms the identification of King Fisherman
with the Pope, and the Great Destruction of
Logres with the Interdict.

In the 'Elucidation,' it is noteworthy that
neither King Arthur nor King Fisherman is
King of Logres. Amangons is King of England. Arthur's knights, indeed, adventure
forth to avenge the wrongs of the Damsels
of the Wells, but they set out not by command
of their King, but in pursuance of a decision
arrived at by a Parliament of their own body.
They are enemies of Amangons; but whatever may be their secret instructions or hostile
intentions towards him, their avowed object
is not to conquer or reconquer England for

Arthur, not to establish or restore its allegiance to him, but simply to find and re-instate the Court of King Fisherman, an object to which the succouring of the Damsels is merely incidental. The situation indicated, perplexing and unintelligible in the romance, becomes not only intelligible, but strictly accurate, when interpreted by history. At the time the Interdict was declared, it will be remembered that Arnold of Cîteaux had been taking counsel with Philip of France as to the policy to be pursued both in Languedoc and England. Innocent was anxious to conclude the Crusade against the Albigenses before declaring a crusade against John, if, indeed, such a crusade should be found necessary. Arnold and Philip, on the other hand, were anxious to convert the Interdict in England at once into a crusade, and to prosecute both Crusades together. This, however, was prevented by the diplomacy of Innocent, and all that Arnold at the time could do was to precipitate the actual infliction of the Interdict, and to induce the General Chapter of Cîteaux—the 'Parliament' referred to—to send a number of preachers into England whose business was to succour the dispossessed clergy and their churches—the Damsels of the Wells. The Crusade against John not being

yet declared, all that the preachers thus sent
could do was to thunder against the iniquities
of John, proclaim the impossibility of restoring
the usual services of the Church until John had
either made full restitution or been deposed,
foment agitation generally, and, in the
meanwhile, exercise and exceed Cistercian privileges during Interdict, by public celebration of
Mass whenever and wherever an opportunity
presented itself. The romancer speaks in
figures, it is true, but somehow he contrives
to convey a truer picture of that disastrous
time than is to be found in the narrative of any
professed historian.

His portrait of Innocent is specially remarkable. He loves the Papacy, but he hates the
Pope. None of the other versions of the story
so much as hint at the sinister trait in Innocent's character to which he gives conspicuous
prominence. ' He could much of nigromancy.'
The very fact, however, that such a charge
should be brought against King Fisherman
suffices to reveal his real identity. For what
else is the indictment but the cry of the ages
against the Church, the one accusation which
rightly or wrongly her friends have urged
against her as insistently as her foes? Is it
not the charge of simony, the traffic in things

spiritual for lucre, the very sin to which the arch-necromancer Simon Magus unwittingly bequeathed his name? Innocent may have been in deed, as in name, innocent of the crime, but he did not escape the charge. It is a contemporary of Innocent who cries against the Church that she

> ' Sets aloft on Peter's throne knaves to keep her under,
> Simon's own apprentices only swift to plunder ';

and years later Matthew Paris, a master in the art of disparagement, is careful to leave the same sin at Innocent's door.

Matthew notes also another characteristic of King Fisherman to which the romancer calls special attention. ' He changed his semblance a hundred times,' says the elucidator. Matthew Paris chimes in with : ' A very various Pope !' —*multum varius Papa*. In his capacity as Fisherman, moreover, Innocent evidently fails to commend himself to the approval of the expounder. He who saw King Fisherman in one guise would never recognise him in another, we are told ; and in simple fact, one who had watched that wary angler for big fish in troubled waters might well be startled to find that the man in the boat was in reality none other than the successor of S. Peter, the Vicar at once of God and humanity. Perhaps, after all, taking into account the natural feelings of a Cistercian writer towards a Pope who had effectually bitted and bridled his Order, it is creditable not to have indulged in more open-mouthed dispraise of Innocent.

The scene in which the King, like the sun of the Psalmist, 'cometh forth like a bridegroom out of his chamber,' needs little comment. It is no temporal monarch that sits crowned at the high table above his knights while the Graal is served to all without servitor or seneschal. We are present at a ceremonial rite even more sacred than the celebration of pontifical High Mass. The voice of lamentation has ceased, and into the hall left void and astonied have thronged 'the Princes of the Churches, the victorious paladins of war, the knighthood of the Court of Heaven, the guiding lights of the world,' in preparation for the holiest Sacrament of all, the Communion of the Church Militant on earth with the Church Triumphant in heaven. No hands are they of man nor angel that serve of the Graal at that transcendent Last Supper, no voice of man nor angel repeats the words, 'Take, eat, this is My body which is given for you.' The secret that the romancer fears to tell is breathed in the far-off chant of the 'choir invisible.'

The mystery of the Graal is the mystery of the Holy Eucharist, and is as fitly expressed in the language of the High History or the Elucidation as in any other. The Blood that flowed from the Saviour's side when pierced by the lance of Longinus falls drop by drop into the Graal, and is there transubstantiated into the wine of the Holy Sacrament. The prohibition of the Sacrament during Interdict is the disappearance of the Graal; the entire removal of Interdict is the full achievement of the Graal; the relaxation of Interdict so far as to allow the Cistercian privilege of celebrating Mass is the adventure of the Graal. If this privilege were allowed, the Blood from the lance of Longinus would still fall drop by drop into the Graal, and the Graal would still be served to the Cistercians and their friends. There is still extant one Latin line which can with absolute certainty be attributed to Walter Mapes, the Archdeacon of Oxford, who is generally credited with being not a mere poet, but a very *Corpus Poetarum*, Latin and French. In this line, as was his inveterate habit, he falls foul of the Cistercians. The rest of the poem is lost—

'Lance of Longinus! White flock! Unspeakable Order!'

The 'white flock' and 'unspeakable Order' refer clearly, as may be gathered from the angry answer of a Cistercian brother to the Archdeacon's taunt, to the white monks of the Order of Cîteaux. The meaning of the nickname 'Lance of Longinus,' whether conferred by Walter or assumed by the Cistercians themselves, is equally obvious. During Interdict the Cistercians, in virtue of their privilege, were the Lance of Longinus from which the Blood still dripped into the Holy Graal.

The Elucidation supplies a still more curious illustration of Cistercian privilege during Interdict. 'The hall that was great and wide remained void and astonied, and the stream of blood ran from the vessel where was the Lance through the rich channel of silver.' At first sight this would seem inconsistent with the sacramental character of the Blood from the Lance of Longinus. In reality, this incidental mention of 'the rich channel of silver' is a striking additional proof of the identity of the Graal with the cup of the Eucharist. The entire passage, it will be observed, refers to a state of Interdict. The void hall, the cries and lamentations repeated thrice daily, point obviously to a time of lamentation and mourn-

ing and woe—in a word, to a time of Interdict,
during which the Cistercians enjoyed the
privilege of celebrating Mass. The apparent
difficulty is solved at once by a reference to
Cistercian usage. According to immemorial
custom, the brethren of Cîteaux partake of the
sacramental wine through a silver tube. The
custom, indeed, was not confined to the Cistercians, nor were the Cistercians monopolists
of the privilege of celebrating during Interdict;
but it is simply a historic fact that wherever
the terms of Interdict were obeyed, no wine
from the Eucharistic cup passed the lips of the
faithful except through 'the rich channel of
silver.' An 'undesigned coincidence' of this
kind seems to me conclusive evidence not only of
the identity of the Graal with the Eucharist, but
of the 'Great Destruction' with the Interdict.

It will not have escaped notice that in the
Elucidation, Perceval is said to have asked
certain questions during his visit to the Castle
of the Graal, of which no mention is made in
the High History. The elucidator records not
only one, but two unasked questions in addition
to several others to which, apparently, Perceval
received satisfactory answers. 'He asked whereof
the Graal served—(*de coi li Gréaus servoit*)—but
demanded not as to the lance when he saw

it, wherefore it should bleed (*por coi sainna*).'
Rendered in the language of history, I take
these words to mean that Dominic, in his inter-
views with Innocent, made careful inquiries
with regard to the doctrine of Transubstantiation, and the legality of treating as heretics
those who dissented from a dogma not yet
declared *de Fide* ; but did not inquire as to the
privilege of celebrating during Interdict. So
far the two accounts tally ; but the elucidator
adds that Perceval also neglected to ask any
question as to ' the Sword whereof the one half
was taken away, and the other lay in the bier
over one dead after the manner of a great
swooning.' The two versions are not inconsistent. The later romance supplies fuller
details, but it confirms the earlier one so far
as relates to the question of privilege. The
unasked question in relation to the Sword only
preserves for us an additional circumstance of
the story. Here, as throughout, history supplies the only intelligible interpretation of the
fiction. King Fisherman falls into 'languishment' on account of the first question not
having been asked. The omission to ask the
second has caused the King of the Lower Folk
to fall into a deadly swoon. He lies there in
the void hall on a bier, like a veritable corpse,

half his sword carried away, the other half with
the hilt lying, like a crucifix, on his breast.
He will rise and grasp and wield the broken
blade to bloody purpose presently, but the
other half will not be welded on as yet. Just
now, Arnold of Cîteaux is in sore disfavour. He
had thought to fight the Crusade in Languedoc
and England at the same time. Half his
sword, the English Crusade, has been broken
off. The other half is only waiting for him to
arise from swoon. If only Dominic had bethought him to ask Innocent to allow the
Cistercians and their allies a free hand in
England as in Languedoc, that sword would
be whole, and that seeming lifeless King leading
the armies of God and Holy Church to victory.
Here, as in the case of the 'languishment' of
King Fisherman and fifty other cases, it has
only to be remembered, in order to render the
narrative clearly intelligible, that the romance
is not a continued allegory, but simply a
sequence of metaphors, often incongruous, and
sometimes conflicting. Metaphors as a rule are
apt to be foundered in the off hind leg, and in
driving a four-in-hand of them the halting of
one is sometimes enough to throw the whole
team out of gear. In this particular instance,
however, there is not even a jumble of

metaphors. The High History makes Perceval omit to ask only one question. The Elucidation makes him omit two. A third or a fiftieth version might make him omit a thousand just as easily. The point of the High Historian is that the omission brought about the English Interdict. The point of the Elucidator is the same, but with the addition that another omission at the same time also brought about another misfortune.

Two additional questions, he further tells us, Perceval remembered to ask: one as to the treasure—*li deniés*—that was in the hall, the other as to the rich cross of silver that came foremost of all. As to the first, I am in doubt what the word *deniés* may mean in this connection. It may perhaps have reference to the 'Peter's pence' collected in England and other countries, to oblations made at Mass, or to a dozen other kinds of offerings known as 'pennies.' The meaning, however, of the passage seems clearly to be that Dominic before starting on his mission came to an understanding with Innocent as to the funds necessary for carrying on the campaign. The rich cross of silver which came foremost I take to be a reference to the Cistercians. The high day of the Order, the annual general meeting of the

Chapter, was September 14, the day of the 'Exaltation of the Cross.' The phrase, in all probability, means nothing more than that Dominic, before undertaking his mission under the wing of the Order, was desirous of ascertaining the position of the Cistercians in relation to the Papacy, and obtained an assurance of the powers that had been intrusted to them in Languedoc.

V

THE CURSE OF LOGRES

Ardentes anime
Flent sine fine:
Ambulant per tenebras
Dicuntque singule:
'Ve! Ve! Ve! quante
Sunt tenebre!'

(MONE. I. 407.)

THE Elucidator's description of the desolation
wrought by the Interdict is metaphorical, no
doubt, but in this case the metaphor is at least
as old as the days of Isaiah, and has long since
passed into the poetic language of all countries:
'The highways lie waste, the wayfaring man
ceaseth; the earth mourneth and languisheth.
Lebanon is ashamed and hewn down; Sharon
is like a wilderness, and Bashan and Carmel
shake off their fruits.' The *trouveur* is well
within his rights when he pictures the Interdict
as the Great Destruction. Nearly seven hundred
years have come and gone since then, and we

Englishmen of to-day, a lay-minded folk much misguided of philosophic historians, find it hard to understand how heavy a curse it was. The following document, every paragraph of which bears the stamp of its authenticity, is, I believe, not referred to by any 'standard historian,' and is here printed in English for the first time. It will be found to convey a far clearer idea of the real suffering inflicted by the Interdict than any extant account of that event. No better commentary can be written on the curse that falls on the realm of Logres in the romances of the Graal :—

'This is the Form of the General Interdict constituted throughout England by Innocent III. on account of the contumacy of John the King.

'That whensoever they will, so it be without solemnity or music of any kind, the clergy may say all the Hours and read the Gospel in the churches, but with doors closed so that no laic may enter, neither for prayer nor otherwise, save it be some powerful person not excommunicated who in all devotion may ask to enter, and whom to repulse might cause grievous injury to the Church. In such case let him then go in alone, but nought let him hear of the priest save the word of preaching, that he is to obey God rather than man, and other the like things.

'Also, let the Chaplains call together their parishioners every Lord's Day and the principal festivals at some cross in the town or in the churchyard, and with all diligence preach to them patience and obedience, how Christ was made obedient to the Father, etc. And let them teach that God is rather to be obeyed than man ; fear not them that have power to kill the body, and the like. When the preaching is done, let the priests most devoutly say prayers for the peace of the Church and for the lord King, that the Lord Jesus Christ may direct his feet into the way of salvation, and give him the spirit of counsel that he may see what things ought to be done according to God, and may be strong to fulfil what he shall see. Let them say prayers, moreover, both for the living and the dead as they have been accustomed, all with bended knees, and let them right diligently admonish the people that by day and night they pray instantly in like manner so that they may supply the want of Masses by vigils and prayers ; for all they that shall be obedient to the Church of God do enter also into the way of salvation, but they that shall prove rebellious may well dread the vengeance of God, for accursed is the child that with his fist resisteth his mother when she scourgeth him.

'Let the Chaplains give notice of feasts, but let them make neither bread nor holy water. Also, let little ones be baptized in the houses with chrism and unction and with all due solemnity. And let all Archdeacons and Deans assemble together on the Day of the Supper as they have been accustomed, and there let it be told them what it may behove them to do; but let the old chrism everywhere be preserved.[1]

[1] Parish priests are often called 'Chaplains,' *capellani*, as having charge of the church or chapel (*v.* Du Cange, *s.v.* 2). The chrism used in baptism—olive-oil impregnated with frankincense—was always made and consecrated on 'the day of the Supper,' Maundy Thursday, in sufficient quantity to last for the year. A Canon of the Council of Meaux in 845 forbids its being made at any other time (*v.* Du Cange, *s.v.* Coena Domini). In John Myrc's *Instruction for Parish Priests,* Early Eng. Text Soc. 1868, p. 20, we read :—

> 'Uche yere ones chawnge thy creme
> And that as sone as thow may
> Anon after Schere Thursday ;
> Thow moste chawnge thyn oyle also . . .'

See also p. 4 of the same tractate. A text, *Imple mandata Domini in coena Ipsius,* seems to have been in very early days quoted as an authority for the practice, and in modern days as having originated the word 'Maundy.' I cannot trace the text, and misdoubt the etymology (*v.* Hampson, Kal. Med. Ævi. *s.v.*)

' Let the parishioners have a common vessel for baptizing children that can be carried from one house to another, but let the water of baptism be honourably set aside, and let the vessel be honourably kept in proper custody.

' Whosoever shall request confession, let him have it whensoever he will, and let him make lawful testament and with all solemnity, but without the Eucharist and without Extreme Unction.

' Let the bodies of the defunct, as well clerics as laics, be placed wheresoever their friends will, without the churchyard, and especially where passers-by may be moved at the sight thereof, but so that no priest be present at the funeral of laics, albeit while the corpse lieth in the house, a priest may privately make commendation of the soul, though without the cross and without holy water.

' Clerics defunct may well be laid aside in sealed trunks or in leaden vessels on the trees of the churchyard or on the wall, and let the bodies of religious be placed within their own precincts without opening the ground of the churchyard. Also let the altars in the churches be made bare.

' Moreover, women shall not be admitted

for purification.   Espousals and marriages may
not be contracted.

‘ Wheresoever ye shall see or hear of violence
done in matters ecclesiastical, ye shall forthwith
cause the damage to be appraised and committed to writing, and the names of such evil-
doers shall ye set down in writing, publicly
denouncing them moreover as excommunicate,
who if they shall repent them, let them be sent
to the Bishop.

‘ Let the masters of schools, if they be per-
mitted of the laity, be received worshipfully,
and let them read and teach.

‘ Moreover, to them that might have received the Body of the Lord and, having notice
that they should receive it, did nevertheless
despise the warning, it is not allowed to eat
flesh-meats without counsel of the Bishop or
some other person having authority, neither on
Easter Day nor thereafter.   Moreover, of this
shall ye give them notice publicly, but without
reproof.

‘ Chapters may be held by the Deans, and as
far as may be crimes as well of clerics as of laics
may be rooted out, but offenders may also be
punished by excommunication.   Moreover, let
the Chapters be held in the churchyards or in
the priests’ houses, and not in the church itself.

'Moreover, saving the person of the lord King, and the Queen, and the person of the Justiciar of the lord King, all the Bishops of England shall solemnly excommunicate any person whosoever that shall lay violent hands on the churches or goods or chattels of clerics, or any that against the will of the clerics shall buy aught of their goods from robbers, or shall receive from the house of evil-doers, or remove, or carry away to take care of the same save with the goodwill of the clerics or on their behalf. This let the Chaplains publicly announce as often as they preach.

'Let the Body of the Lord, wheresoever any shall have been left over, be worshipfully preserved in the church until it shall be declared what is to be done with it, so that it be taken of none, neither priest nor other.

'Let the clergy store their goods in the churches and churchyards, that so by God's gift they shall there have peace.

'If the days of the Hospitallers shall betide, let the priests diligently admonish the people to come together without the church to their preaching, and most devoutly pay heed to the Brotherhood; but let the doors of the church not be opened to them, nor let them be allowed to bury any person in the churchyard, but

otherwise in whatsoever manner they may, let
the clerics manifest them their helpers, and let
the priests point out to them that this Interdict
is of the lord Pope whom none may resist.   So
general is it and so stringent that no privilege
nor permission of Masses nor of no other liberties
can be observed.   Let the parishioners nevertheless be held to the payment of alms and fulfilment of promises lest God on account of their
hardness be the more hardly wroth with them ;
and when God shall give peace to the Church,
all things shall be repaid alike to quick and
dead.

'Fugitives also, whosoever shall flee for
refuge to the peace of the Church, let them be
admitted to the protection of the Church.

' It is allowed to use blessings at meat and to
say grace as usual.   Farewell.' [1]

---

[1] Martène, Thes. Anecd. i. 812, from a MS. of 'S. Michael
in Peril of the Sea,' *i.e.* Mont S. Michel in Normandy.   It is
reprinted in Migne, Patrol. Op. Innoc. III. vol. iv. col. 190, and
in Dumont, Corpus univ. dipl. I. i. 385.   It is referred to in
Potthast, Reg. i. 286, under date March 22, 1208.

The Knights Hospitallers every year sent preachers round the
country to collect subscriptions for the hospital at Jerusalem.
They were entitled by their privilege to hold a service once a
year in any parish church for the purpose, and these ' days of
the Hospitallers ' were generally observed as high holidays in the
towns they visited.   Their preachers were eloquent, and the
indulgences granted to those that gave alms were large.   The

Such is the ' form ' of the Interdict, and such in the main was the substance. Perhaps no other legal document in the world contains a gallery of pictures at once so vivid, so various, and so sombre. The ' powerful person ' whom to gainsay might be a grievous harm to the clergy, entering the disgarnished church at his castle gates alone, and then only to hear the preacher rolling out his solemn denunciations —the parish priest, if indeed he be not the king's prisoner in his own parsonage, crying aloud his jeremiads at the market-cross, and giving notice of festivals that cannot be observed —the baptisms in the portable fonts in private houses—the anguish and terror of the dying penitent as he turned his face to the wall, not un-houselled, indeed, but disappointed and unaneled —the despair and indignation of lover and lass forbidden to consecrate their love by union in holy matrimony—the compassion of passers-by moved by the sight of the coffined or uncoffined corpses that fringed the highway, the ' sealed trunks ' on the churchyard walls, and the ' leaden

---

abuse of their privileges was a frequent cause of scandal in the Church. The founder of our modern ' Hospital Sunday,' the late Mr. T. B. Wright of Birmingham, was probably unaware of the antiquity of the custom he revived.

vessels' among the branches of the yew-trees,—
all these and a hundred other shapes of misery
rise before us as we read—a phantasmagory of
suffering undeserved, in which the most honest
and religious, the wisest and the best of the community, are called on to undergo a martyrdom
that falls more lightly on the thoughtless ne'er-
do-weel, the scoffer, the hypocrite, and the
knave.

No doubt the degree of severity with which
the Interdict was enforced varied to some
extent in the different dioceses, archdeaconries,
and parishes. The provision, in reference to
betrothals and marriages more particularly,
seems to have been frequently construed in a
sense less subversive of public morality than the
bare words of the ' form ' might seem to imply.
If, in spite of ecclesiastical prohibition, Robin
and Marion ventured to 'contract' espousal
and matrimony, and declared themselves ready
to undergo any penance that might be enjoined
for the infringement of the Interdict, there
was nothing in the actual letter of the law to
prevent Robin giving Marion a wedding-ring
at the church-door, nothing to prevent a kindly
Father Gervase or Brother Bernard pronounc-
ing them man and wife, or whispering a
blessing on their union. The sin lay with

the contracting parties, and in most cases, probably, was capable of being compounded for on terms considerably short of generally prohibitive.

It would be a mistake, however, to assume that there was any general laxity in the enforcement of the Interdict, at least during the earlier years of its infliction. The interest, not only of the spiritual power, but of the hostile temporal power, lay, or was supposed to lie, in making the Interdict absolutely intolerable. Innocent's object was to coerce John, John's to coerce Innocent. When John found it impossible to counteract the Interdict by the issue of royal edicts and ordinances forbidding its observance, he adopted the policy of redoubling its severity with a view to exasperating the nobility and the people against the tyranny of the Church. He celebrated, for instance, his Christmas at Bristol in 1209 by forbidding the national sports of hunting and hawking, and at the same time throwing down the fences and filling up the ditches round the royal forests, to the ruin of all crops and the general devastation of the country for thousands of square miles. He had sacked the revenues of the Church, and kept the clergy close prisoners in their own parsonages. He had thrown into gaol, not without a dash of grim Angevin humour, all those flesh-and-blood Damsels of the Wells who acted as housekeepers to a nominally celibate clergy, and demanded exorbitant blackmail for setting them at liberty. But he was determined that the Court of King Fisherman and its hangers-on should not be the only sufferers. Not an earl should hunt in the forest, not a churl should dance at a fair. Always sordid, butcherly, and treacherous, he twisted the Interdict into a licence to loot his subjects at large, and the personal excommunication that followed on the heels of the Interdict into a full release from all the obligations of humanity. Measured by the amount of physical and moral suffering inflicted on the community, not the anarchy in the days of Stephen, not the Norman Conquest itself, can be compared with the Curse that fell on Logres from Land's End to the Border during the Interdict in the reign of John.

There is no need to linger over the details of the Interdict either in history or romance. Month after month the years went by, and the duel *à outrance* between Pope and King was still maintained inexorably and implacably by both combatants. From the first, Arnold of

Cîteaux had done all that any King of the Lower Folk could do to convert the Interdict into a Crusade. Sorely against his will, but compelled by what seemed to be the absolute necessity of the case, Innocent finally yielded to the pressure directly and indirectly brought to bear upon him by Arnold. He excommunicated John personally, released his subjects from their allegiance, proclaimed a Crusade against him, and specially commissioned Philip of France to undertake the congenial task of carrying out the Crusade by the conquest of England. Hardly was the mandate issued before Innocent saw how fatal was the blunder to which he had committed himself.

The dearest wish of his heart was to unite the princes of Christendom against the paynims of Palestine. Thanks to the force of circumstances and Arnold of Cîteaux, he now found himself involved in three separate Crusades against three Christian potentates. The three were Raymond of Toulouse, John of England, and the now excommunicated Emperor Otho. All three were closely connected by family bonds and many common political interests. All three were enemies whose downfall was necessary to the ambitions of Philip of France. A far less wary pilot than Innocent must have seen the breakers ahead towards which the bark of Peter was drifting so ominously. With but a few comparatively insignificant exceptions, Philip had already wrested from John all his continental dominions, and the Albigensian Crusade had practically established his sovereignty in the South of France. Philip as conqueror of England must inevitably be to all practical intents the Dictator, possibly the acknowledged Emperor, of Western Christendom. With the declaration of a crusade against John, the practical control and direction of ecclesiastical affairs in England passed out of the hands of Innocent and the Interdict Commissioners into those of Arnold of Cîteaux, the usual and recognised Chief of the Papal executive into whose department naturally fell all matters connected with Crusade. Innocent, it seems clear, who knew that Arnold had his hands full in Languedoc, had not calculated the possible results of the Abbot's hostility in relation to the English Interdict. He now began to realise that he could no more rely on the Order of Cîteaux than on the Abbot. The Order was loyal to Arnold, and Arnold was loyal to Philip of France. The Roman Aaron, in fact, felt that he had commissioned a mutinous Moses to act in the interests of a

French Pharaoh, and that the Cistercian children of Israel were disposed to follow Moses rather than Aaron.

By a strange and strangely momentous coincidence of unlikely events, the liberties of England, won by the efforts of the French Abbot to counteract the policy of the Pope, were secured and confirmed by the efforts of the Italian Pope to counteract the policy of the Abbot. The histories which tell us how the sealing of Magna Charta was wrung from John by the ' Army of God and Holy Church ' all fail to tell us that this is the official title of a crusading army and none other. All fail to tell us that the invasion of England attempted and in great part carried out by Philip's son Lewis was part and parcel of the same Crusade, and that from the moment of John's submission to Innocent the Crusade was carried on by the Cistercians and their allies in the teeth of Innocent's denunciations. They fail to tell us, moreover, that the army which finally drove Lewis out of England and established Henry of Winchester on the throne was also a crusading army, and that in this case the Crusade was forced by Innocent on the recalcitrant Cistercians, whom he compelled to undo the work of their own hands, to accept the policy of Rome, and to renounce the policy of Cîteaux.

As far as I can judge, Innocent's urgent appeals to John to admit Stephen Langton, and at a later period to become a homager of Rome, were dictated by a sincere desire to save John in spite of himself, not for John's own sake, but for the sake of the Papacy; and I fail to see in what manner he could have interfered effectively without securing in the first place a clear right according to feudal law and custom to interfere at all. The moment that John laid his crown at Pandulph's feet and became the liegeman of the Pope, Innocent was not merely justified in championing his cause—he was bound in feudal honour so to do. That in fighting his vassal's battle he fought for his own hand; that in the course of the fight he cursed Magna Charta, excommunicated the barons, suspended the 'patriot' Archbishop, and played havoc generally with the parchment constitution and its propounders cleric and lay, is no doubt true. That the liberties of England were really at stake; that the conflict between John and the barons was the supreme crisis of English freedom, is also true. None the less true is it that those liberties were far safer in the hands of Innocent than in those of the

' patriot ' barons who, despairing of the republic,
' sought for a new King, and sought for him
beyond the sea.' None the less true is it that
if from that day to this our freedom has broad-
ened slowly down from precedent to precedent,
we owe it to 'the interference of an Italian
priest' in the darkest hour of our peril. We
may hold that the conquest of England by
Lewis, even if it had been successful, could in
the nature of things have been only temporary ;
but at least let us take off our hats gratefully
and reverently to the Roman statesman who
saved us from that threatened humiliation.

The Interdict was solemnly dissolved on
June 29, 1214. Two years later, July 16,
1216, Innocent died in the midst of the great
battle that still raged in England, and his death
suspended for a time the active measures he
had taken to prevent the projected invasion of
England either by Philip or his son Lewis.
Innocent's successor, Honorius III., inherited
his policy, if not his genius ; and happily
Arnold of Cîteaux had now for some few years
become Archbishop, and, more questionably,
Duke of Narbonne, a rise in dignity coupled
with a loss of political power which materially
altered his views of men and things. On his
promotion, the most influential personage at

the Cistercian Round Table, although in technical strictness not a Cistercian himself, was Stephen Langton ; but Stephen's influence had been to a great extent paralysed by the suspension of his archiepiscopal functions, a sentence which not only impaired his authority, but involved his absence from the scene of action on a journey to Rome. Innocent's death precipitated and assisted the enterprise of Lewis; and by the time that the Papal legate Gualo arrived in England, London and a great part of the country were already in the hands of the French invader and his allies the King of Scotland and the 'patriot' barons. But Honorius was resolute, and Gualo was a capable and devoted lieutenant. The kingdom of Scotland and those parts of England which acknowledged the sovereignty of the French Prince were at once laid under Interdict. Then came the death of John, a fortunate event for which the Cistercians claimed, and perhaps deserved, the credit. A little later followed the new Crusade against Lewis, Gualo himself being the first to take the cross. Then followed the 'Fair of Lincoln,' the defeat and departure of Lewis, and the final allegiance of the barons to Henry of Winchester, Pecorins the son of Amangons, the sheepish son of a wolfish father.

The words of the Elucidation in reference
to the events here referred to are worth careful
attention: 'This King Arthur of whom I
speak held war against the folk of his land four
years.' The romancer, clearly, is not speaking
of the well-known traditional King Arthur of
Britain, who is nowhere recorded to have held
war against the folk of his land. The Arthur
of whom he speaks is an Arthur who makes
war on Britain for four years, and is not
successful after all. The war is over at the
time the romancer is writing. 'But all this
draweth to an end, so that no man nor neighbour was there that did not his will therein,
either of force or of goodwill.' King Arthur
has not conquered Britain, but his own people
and their neighbours are on terms of peace, and
the King of Logres is anxious to maintain
friendship with Arthur and to avoid giving him
any cause of offence. It was in the first days
of 1214 that the Crusade of Philip against
John was solemnly promulgated. It was in
the first days of 1218 that Philip finally renounced his intention of invading England.
In the autumn of 1217, after the crushing defeat
at Lincoln, Philip's son Lewis had sworn to
depart with his Frenchman from England
never to return. He had promised further to

do all that lay in his power to induce his father
to respect the rights of the young Henry of
Winchester in his dominions oversea. He had
been granted an alms of £5000 by the City of
London to relieve his pressing necessities, and
had been conducted to Dover by the Earl
Marshal. He had returned to his father's court
defeated and disgraced ; but it was not till the
beginning of 1218 that it was known for
certain in England that Philip would acquiesce
in the failure of the enterprise on which he had
staked so much, and allow the realm of Logres to
re-establish peace and order within its frontiers
undisturbed by enemies from without.

When he speaks of King Arthur holding
war for four years against the folk of his land,
the elucidator is explicit enough in his reference,
but has his reasons for reticence as to the later
episodes of the story. He has no such reasons
when he comes to describe the concluding
scenes of the Interdict itself. On the very
day the Court and the rich Meinie were set
free, the folk of the land went a-hunting in the
forest, and they that would fain go a-hawking
followed the good rivers. Nought did they
but make merry the winter through until the
summer. The actual release from the Interdict
took place on June 29, 1214, after the curse

had lasted, as the chroniclers are careful to record, six years, three months, and fourteen days, but John's retaliatory ordinances had been repealed some months before. Nicholas, Cardinal Bishop of Tusculum, and Legate of the Holy See, had been despatched by Innocent in the autumn of 1213 to ratify and confirm what had been already done by the envoy Pandulph, and to conclude all matters in relation to the Interdict as ambassador-plenipotentiary. John received him with all honour, repeated his oath of fealty, did homage for his kingdom, and made the first payment of a thousand marks to his acknowledged feudal lord. It was at this time that John formally revoked his edicts against hunting and hawking, and that those whose sporting instincts were stronger than their regard for ecclesiastical proprieties found themselves once more free to enjoy their favourite pastimes. The romancer evidently felt that sport of any kind was a thing to be sternly discountenanced during Interdict. He recounts the lamentable fact that hunting and hawking did actually take place to the shame of the folk of Logres, and counts abstention from the sports of the field for righteousness to the folk of Arthur, but he is not disposed to seem unreasonably austere. Some men are

made that way. Everybody is not a Cistercian,
and it takes some of all sorts, even sportsmen
and dandies, to make a world. To the reader
of to-day, the striking point in the narrative is
that it is obviously written while the circumstances were still freshly remembered. 'Most
of ye know,' says the *Trouveur*, 'that these things
were so.' He is no retailer of forgotten or
half-forgotten legends. He is simply bearing
witness to a matter of public notoriety in the
presence of an audience to whom he can appeal
to check and verify his statements. We may
safely accept it as a historic fact, albeit elsewhere unrecorded, that there were folk in
England who took advantage of the revoca-
tion of John's edicts in the late autumn of
1213 to make merry the winter through till
the relaxation of the Interdict itself in the
summer of 1214.

VI

ARTHUR

Ecce Judas alter, Herodes ecce secundus,
Qui pueros inter Messiam perdere querens
Ne regnum perdat, proprios occidere natos
Postea non veritus, et regnum perdidit et se.
Sic tibi continget Arthuri morte, Johannes!
Ejus per vitam metuisti perdere regnum,
Ejus per mortem vita regnoque carebis!

(PHILIPPIS, vi.)

IT will have been observed not only that the
King Arthur of the Graal legend is not the
traditional King Arthur of Geoffry of Monmouth, but that in some way 'this King
Arthur' of whom the *Trouveur* speaks is
identified with King Philip of France. The
process by which the Breton or British legendary
hero was transmuted into a French monarch is
not only capable of a simple and easy expla-
nation, but vividly illustrates the accuracy of
the general hypothesis here propounded.

When Richard I. of England died, the young

Prince Arthur, son of Richard's brother Geoffry, had a rightful claim to succeed his uncle in all his dominions in preference to Richard's brother John, who was younger than Geoffry. This claim, recognised by the feudal common law of Christendom, was only legally and constitutionally defeasible by the Great Councils of England, Normandy, and the other great fiefs which Richard had held. In the legal exercise of their functions, the Great Council of England promptly decided to set aside the hereditary claim of Arthur in favour of the remoter hereditary claim of John, and from that moment Arthur's perfectly valid inchoate right to the Crown of England absolutely ceased and determined in law.

In Normandy and the other great fiefs oversea the case was different. The Great Councils, in theory at least, had the same right of setting aside the next heir in favour of one more remote, but the right was conditional, not absolute. The Dukes of Normandy were 'men' of the Kings of France; and before any claimant could legally be invested with the Duchy, he was bound to do homage and swear fealty to the French King, who, on sufficient cause shown in his own High Court, had a right to veto the election of the Norman

Baronage. Richard died April 6, 1199. On the 25th, John had been girt with the sword and crowned with the coronet of Normandy, 'entwined with little golden roses,' at Rouen, and had made solemn oath on the Holy Gospels before clergy and people that he would maintain the rights of Mother Church, exercise right justice, do away bad laws and institute good. But he was not yet lawful Duke of Normandy. Philip of France lost no time in reminding him of the fact by provisionally receiving homage from Arthur not only for Normandy, but for Anjou, Poitou, Maine, and Touraine as well as Brittany. Philip, however, was at this time fighting with only his left hand free, his right being engaged in his duel with the Papacy on the question of his marriage. In the spring of 1200, he was fain to make peace with John, admitting him to do homage and swear fealty for Normandy and the other fiefs as the rightful heir of Richard.

It was John's marriage with Isabella of Angoulême that determined the manner of his doom. Isabella had long been betrothed to Hugh le Brun, Count of la Marche, but even yet had scarcely reached an age to be married in the face of the Church. John, who had divorced his first wife Hawise of Gloucester,

on the ground of consanguinity, had sent an
embassy to Lisbon to demand the hand of the
Infanta of Portugal. Before his envoys had
returned, he had seen and been smitten with an
infatuated passion for Isabella, and both the
unfulfilled contracts were forthwith flung to
the winds. The King of Portugal complained,
Hugh of la Marche threatened. John carried
off his bride, and was solemnly crowned a
second time with her at Westminster, October
8, 1200.

The next year saw John and Isabella sump-
tuously lodged in Philip's own palace at Paris,
and Philip ostentatiously showering gifts of
wines and embroideries, Spanish destriers and
rich jewels, on his royal and amorous guests.
It was not thus that Philip treated his friends.
In this year (1201) Hugh le Brun complained
to Philip of the outrage John had committed
in carrying off his affianced bride, and a
number of others who had suffered wrong at
the hands of John appealed to John's over-lord
for vengeance and protection. Philip accordingly summoned John as his liegeman for
Anjou, Poitou, Aquitaine, and Touraine to
appear at his Court in Paris on the second
Sunday after Easter 1202 to answer the charges
brought against him.

The Court met, but John did not appear.
The Dukes of Normandy might be bound to
appear on the citation of the Kings of France,
but only on the march between kingdom and
duchy—not at Paris. Finally, the Court found
John guilty of contumacy for his non-appear-
ance, and sentenced him to confiscation of all
the lands which he or his predecessors had held
of the Kings of France. Whether the Court
was legally justified in passing this sentence,
or Philip in at once proceeding to execute it,
are questions which after-events very soon
deprived of any practical interest or importance. If the sentence and its execution were
legal, they were confirmed; if illegal, they
were superseded by a second sentence, the
legality of which in all essential respects, as
legality was understood at the time, seems to
be indisputable.

The story of Prince Arthur's capture at
Mirebeau, his imprisonment at Falaise and
Rouen, and his final disappearance about Easter
1203, is too well known to need repetition.
That John murdered him with his own hand
seems on the whole to be the likeliest story of
his death. That directly or indirectly John
was guilty of murdering his nephew is absolutely certain. The murder afforded Philip

an admirable opportunity of re-asserting his
title in such a form as to render it legally
unassailable. Nothing should be left undone
that could secure his lawful right at least to
the England oversea. Arthur had died Count
of Brittany. A meeting of the Great Council
of Brittany was therefore necessary. Arthur
died homager to Philip, and his death involved
questions of the highest moment to the realm
of France. A meeting of the Great Council
of the realm therefore became necessary.
Arthur died under circumstances of which the
Court of Rome claimed the right of taking
cognisance. The meeting of a Legatine
Council therefore became necessary. Three
meetings were held accordingly—one of the
Great Council of Brittany at Vannes on
April 18, 1203 ; one of the Great Council of
France at Mantes on August 22, 1203 ; and
one of a Council summoned by the Papal
Legate at Meaux in the late spring or early
summer of 1204.

Both the date and the place of meeting of
the Great Council of France seem to be significant. John had pleaded as his excuse for not
appearing when cited the year before that the
notice given was insufficient, and that the
Dukes of Normandy were not bound to appear

when cited by the Kings of France except on
the frontiers of the duchy and the kingdom.
In this case, accordingly, the notice given seems
to have been three months, three weeks, and
three days, and the place chosen was one where
a meeting could easily be arranged on the
bridge over the Seine between Mantes and
Limay, without requiring Duke or King to set
foot within his enemy's territory.

There were many counts in the indictment
against John, and the record of the proceedings
is fragmentary and incomplete. The general
outline of the case, however, is distinctly trace-
able. John was accused of 'that worst kind
of homicide which is called murder.' He was
found guilty and sentenced to death. This
sentence carried with it the forfeiture of all
his goods and possessions in France to the
Crown of France. But Philip was not merely
the sovereign to whom the belongings of the
murderer were forfeit. He was also the rightful successor to the belongings of the murdered
man. Arthur was his 'man' in respect of
many fiefs; and Arthur dying without heirs,
the fiefs escheated to Philip as his lord. A
third point raised before the Great Council
related, not to the actual possessions of either
John or Arthur, but to the allegiance of the

vassals who held under them. One of the articles in the last peace concluded between Philip and John had provided that if either of them should break the peace against the other, the liegemen of the party so breaking it should be *ipso facto* absolved from their allegiance to him. The murder of Arthur was held to be against the peace of our lord King Philip, his crown and dignity, and consequently all of John's 'men' were held to be thereby released from their allegiance to John.

John refused to appear before the Great Council in person, but he seems to have been represented at it, probably, I think, by the Papal Legate or one or more of those attached to the Papal Legation. The defence, apparently, was a plea of 'confession and avoidance.' The homicide was not denied, but it was urged that it did not amount to murder. Arthur had been taken in arms against his liege lady, his grandmother Eleanor, and his liege lord, his uncle King John. Under such circumstances, for the liege lord to kill his rebellious vassal, even by a secret and shameful death, was not murder according to the accepted feudal code. This view of the law applicable to this particular case is distinctly laid down by no less accomplished a lawyer than Innocent himself a dozen years later, when the legality of the sentence passed was again under discussion, and may be regarded as technically correct. The Great Council, however, thought fit to override the objection, and it would, perhaps, be as difficult in theory as it was impossible in practice to question their competence to do so. Other pleas were advanced; that John had not been summoned to the Council; that he had not been tried by his peers; that he was condemned in his absence; that even assuming him to have been contumacious in not appearing, the punishment of contumacy was not death, but the loss of the fief or some minor penalty. All these, however, were little better than mere quibbles. The question for the Council to decide was whether the crime committed by John was murder, and they decided that it was.

What Philip regarded as included in the forfeiture and escheat is left indefinite in such records of the trial as have come down to us. That he interpreted the sentence as conferring on himself a rightful claim to the Crown of England as well as to John's dominions oversea seems to be clear. The annalist of Margam tells us how Philip summoned John to his court according to the wont of the Dukes of Nor-

mandy to answer for the slaying of so great a
man as Arthur, and adds: 'So great a man, I
say, for he was the legitimate heir of England,
Count of Brittany, and son-in-law of the King
of France.' The statement that Arthur was
the legitimate heir of England was inaccurate
after John's election by the Great Council, and
the statement that he was Philip's son-in-law
was inaccurate, inasmuch as Arthur was betrothed only, not actually married, to Mary of
France. Both inaccuracies, however, bear
witness to the wish of the Cistercian chronicler
to make the most of the claims of Philip as
the representative of Arthur. He nevertheless
distinctly negatives the supposition that the
Crown of England was declared forfeit by the
Council. 'John,' he says, 'was condemned
by the judgment of the King's Court and of
the French Princes, and was disinherited with
all his heirs of all the lands and honours he
held of the Crown of France. This was
the sentence awarded, and a just sentence
it was.'

The justice of the sentence, however, did
not commend itself to Innocent's Legates or to
Innocent himself, and a determined effort was
made to interpose an appeal to the Court of
Rome on the subject. Philip, at imminent risk

of being excommunicated by Innocent, maintained that no appeal could lie from a decision
of the Great Council of France to the Roman
Curia, and at once set about the execution of
the sentence. Up to this time he had been
executing, as far as lay in his power, the sentence of 1202 against John. Both sentences
were to all practical intents and purposes
identical. The difference was that he now
resumed as the avenger of Arthur the task he
had undertaken as the avenger of Hugh de la
Marche and other of his aggrieved vassals, the
thoroughly congenial task of driving John out
of France. All John's liegemen oversea were
now released from their allegiance, and John
himself was formally branded as the murderer
of his own kith and kin. The sentence had
the effect, and more than the effect, of excommunication. It legalised rebellion against John,
while it paralysed his powers of resistance.
The extraordinary rapidity and ease with which
Philip carried out the sentence of confiscation
bears witness not only to his skill as a general,
but to a widespread popular belief in the righteousness of his cause. Probably it was well for
him that John gave him no opportunity of
carrying out the sentence of death as well as
that of confiscation.

By the time that the Legatine Council was held at Meaux in 1204, with a view to bringing about a peace between Philip and John, Philip had already given practical effect to the sentence of forfeiture. A decision of the Council, however, seems to have been arrived at favourable to the claims of John in reference to Poitou, and perhaps to other of his former possessions. On this occasion, Philip himself interposed an appeal to the Court of Rome. He had refused to allow an appeal from his own Great Council to Rome; but an appeal from a Papal Council to the Pope himself was well in accordance with law, and, moreover, he was now able to base his appeal not only on the righteousness of his cause, but on the logic of events. The appeal was never formally heard. There was no occasion to hear it. Some months after the Council at Meaux, the Archbishop of Rouen applied to Innocent for instructions. Philip, he writes, who is now King, has received homage and fealty from the barons and lay-folk all, and alleges that he has acquired Normandy in pursuance of the sentence of his Court. What are we poor Churchmen to do? Innocent answers his dear bewildered brother on March 7, 1205: You know the facts better probably than I. Act accordingly as you think best in the interests of the Church.

Normandy, in fact, to say nothing of John's other continental fiefs, was already once more part and parcel of France. Philip had won it, and he had won it fairly. According to feudal law, custom, and tradition as understood and accepted at the time, he was now as rightfully King of Normandy as he was King of France. After the death of Richard of England, Philip had accepted homage and fealty from Arthur for Normandy and other of Richard's fiefs. He subsequently found it expedient to divest Arthur of his temporary vassalage to himself, and to invest John with the great continental fiefs. He did so, however, only under practical compulsion and against his will. As soon as John's marriage to Isabella of Angoulême had given just ground of complaint to Hugh de la Marche, and John's other outrages on others of his vassals had driven them into making common cause with Hugh, Arthur again became an invaluable stalking-horse for Philip's designs. The decree of 1202, which declared all John's continental possessions forfeit, was virtually a declaration of Arthur's right to them, and of Philip's determination to vindicate that right. At the very outset of his final conquests from John, Philip was already the representative, the champion knight, of Arthur.

The decision of the Court at Mantes in 1203 laid a still more significant emphasis on the fact. Arthur was murdered. John was the murderer, Philip the avenger of Arthur. It was Arthur's right that John had usurped and had forfeited. It was Arthur's right that now vested in Philip, and that Philip would vindicate. It was Arthur's right for which Philip fought, Arthur's right in which he made conquest after conquest of the dominions that should have been Arthur's, Arthur's right in which he re-united them to the sovereignty of France. A little later, the Albigensian Crusade would give him the opportunity of asserting in Languedoc those rights of Arthur which Arthur's uncle Richard and grandfather Henry had been so solicitous to maintain ; and a few years later yet, Philip by his son Lewis would claim in Arthur's right, and well-nigh succeed in winning, the sovereignty of England itself. Philip and Philip's men, Prelates and Princes of France, Dukes and Counts, and Viscounts and Lords, Arnold of Cîteaux and his invincible brotherhood of Cistercian Abbots, the Barons of England who have renounced their allegiance to John,—they are all now Knights of Arthur.

Their Chiefs, cleric and lay, are the Paladins of a new Table Round. For all of them the name of Arthur is more than the memorial of a crime they have sworn to avenge. It is the symbol of a mystery, the watchword of a Cause.

In both the Greater and the Lesser Britain the name of Arthur had been already consecrated in immemorial tradition. His young Plantagenet namesake was now definitely identified in the popular imagination with the mysterious Breton and British Emperor. The nameless but almost contemporary Canon of Barnwell who supplemented the history of Walter of Coventry writes of the murdered Prince: 'The Bretons, as it were taking augury from the name, continually made it their boast, as impudent as it was imprudent, that in him the ancient Arthur had again been brought to life, and that the slaughter of the English and the transfer of the sovereignty through him to the Bretons was already imminent.' This is evidently the original source of Speed's account: 'The Britaines then, fascinated with his ominous Name, dreamed that the ancient Great Arthur was risen againe in him, and that the Translation of the English Kingdome was now by him to be effected.' Nor was the name the only coincidence. Walter of Coventry himself writes : 'Arthur in the prison of his uncle King John of England, by what chance is doubtful, was done away from the midst, nor, as it is said, hath his sepulchre been found unto this day.'

Many of those who wrought and fought for Philip and Lewis doubtless believed in all good faith that the murdered Prince was none other than the old-world Arthur reborn into the world of living men. Many more shared Philip's presentiments of a united France and his aspirations towards the Empire of Christendom. For the former, the Arthur whom the then present generation had seen and known was the Arthur of the past ; for the latter, the Arthur of the future. To the Order of Cîteaux, to the patriot Barons of England who 'sought for a new king, and sought for him beyond the sea,' the royal soul of the great Arthur might well seem for a little space to have returned from Avalon clad in the outward semblance of Lewis the son of Philip of France.

One connecting link between the Prince Arthur of history and the King Arthur of romance may perhaps be found in the posthumous history of Prince Arthur's sister Eleanor. An anonymous continuation of the Brut of Wace,

printed by F. Michel, records that she was kept
in prison during the whole reign of John, and
that after his death Henry III. sent her from
one place of captivity to another until her death
at Bristol. She was first buried in the Priory
of S. James in that city ; but afterwards, by the
King's desire, her remains were translated to
Amesbury. Whether the translation suggested
to romancers a connection of Amesbury with the
story of Arthur and Guenievre, or whether, as is
more probable, the connection between Amesbury and the Arthurian story suggested to Henry
the choice of her last resting-place, is a question
of little importance. In either case, the fact
bears witness to the recognition of some connection between the legendary and the historic
Arthurs.

VII

DATES

L'en ne doit Crestien de Troies
Ce m'est vis pas raison blasmer,
Qui sot dou roi Artu conter,
De sa cour et de sa mesniée
Qui tant fu loée et prisiée,
Et qui les fez des autres conte,
Et onques de lui ne tient conte :
Trop ert preudon à oblier.

(*Dou Chevalier à l'Espée*, MÉON i. 128.)

IT is beyond my present purpose to point out
the many historical persons and events that
masquerade, often in the slightest of disguises,
through the many versions of the Graal legends.
They will nearly all be found to be closely
connected with the Albigensian Crusades,
the Interdict and Crusade against John of
England, the Crusade and war against the
Emperor Otho terminating with the battle of
Bouvines, and the final Crusade against Philip
and Lewis for the purpose of maintaining the
independence, and indeed the very political

existence, of England as a European power.
There are episodes referring to other events—
some, indeed, that are merely *trouveur* stories
or Dominican 'examples' woven with more or
less skill into the narrative; but the greater part
of the earlier versions will be found to be nothing more nor less than contemporary history
in metaphor.   If the knights of Arthur are
sought for in the ranks of the 'soldierhood of
Christ' that fought on the side of the Cistercians
and Philip of France, the task of identification
will not be found difficult by those acquainted
with the original records of the time.

Two identifications, however, may here be
indicated by way of illustration—that of Lancelot with the elder Simon de Montfort, and that
of Galahad with Francis of Assisi.   The proofs
of these identifications I do not propose to
adduce.   They will be found in plenty, those
in reference to Lancelot more particularly in
the earlier versions of the story, those referring
to Galahad in the later exclusively, as it is only in
these that his name appears at all.   The name
of Lancelot, as of Gawain, figures in Arthurian
romance before the date at which the parent
river received the mighty tributary stream of
the Graal legend.   This fact, however, in no
way militates against the accuracy of the iden-

tifications suggested. The original writers of
the Perceval legends were led partly by the
coincidence of name and partly by other considerations into accepting King Arthur as the
metaphorical name of Prince Lewis of France,
and all that Prince Lewis represented or was
supposed to represent by those who fought for
his cause. But obviously the romancer could
not stop here. If he adopted King Arthur at
all, he must adopt also all the well-known
characters in previous fiction connected with
King Arthur. If he found in earlier Arthurian
romance a character like that of Lancelot, he
would naturally cast about among the living
men whose adventures he proposed to relate
to find one whom he could fitly describe under
the name of Lancelot without violating any
special characteristics by which the elder hero
had been distinguished in popular fiction. The
adventures in which the new Lancelot would
figure would be mostly themselves new, and
new traits would be added to the character in
order to render the portrait more lifelike, but
the general outline would not be altered in any
material respect. The very conditions under
which the new romance would be written
would necessarily involve a distinct similarity
between the new character drawn from life and

the old character drawn from imagination, whatever difference in detail might be introduced.

The identification of Galahad with S. Francis of Assisi really offers the only intelligible key to the most remarkable modification introduced into the legend of the Graal. In all the earlier versions, Perceval is the principal hero of the story. In all the later, Perceval is relegated to a secondary though still honourable place, and Galahad the High Prince is assigned an almost divine pre-eminence. Dominic and Francis are almost exact contemporaries. Dominic's apostolic career began a little earlier than that of Francis ; but at the Lateran Council of 1215, that other disciple did outrun Dominic, and the Order of S. Francis was formally established by Innocent, while the Order of S. Dominic, approved by Innocent, was only formally established by Innocent's successor Honorius. The earlier versions of the Graal legend were, it seems to me, obviously written by partisans of Dominic and the Cistercians. The later versions seem to me as obviously the work of partisans of Francis. The rivalry between Dominican and Franciscan is reflected with striking and impressive accuracy in the differences between the earlier and the later versions, and the temporary waning of the star of Dominic

before the star of Francis from about the year
1218 onwards is as clearly legible in the
modifications of the legend as in any other
record of the time.

Dominic, as we have seen, was Knight of a
Table Round at which sat a King of France
among his princes, and dukes, and prelates,
abbots and monks, preachers and fighters, great
men and masterful, grave men and holy, all
intent on eradicating heresy and remodelling
the politics of Christendom. Francis tells us
that he himself was a Knight of another Table
Round of a somewhat different kind. His
words are : 'My brethren of the Table Round
are they that hide them in the wilderness and in
lonely places that they may give them the more
diligently to prayer and meditation, bewailing
their own sins and those of others, living simply
and conversing humbly, they whose holiness is
known of God albeit at times unknown of their
brethren and of men. The souls of such, what
time they shall be presented by the angels of
the Lord, then shall the Lord show them the
fruit and wages of their labours, to wit, many
souls that have been saved by their examples,
prayers, and tears, and shall say unto them :
" My well-beloved sons, such and so many souls
have been saved through your prayers, and

tears, and examples, and forasmuch as ye have
been faithful over a few things, I will make
ye rulers over many things!"' Was Francis
thinking of the Round Table of an Arthur or
a Charlemagne when he spoke thus, or of that
other Round Table of which his friend and
spiritual brother Dominic was one of the foremost champions?

The actual dates that can be assigned to the
various versions of the Graal legend are few,
but these few are fairly certain. Apart from
indications in the manuscripts of the legend
themselves, the one cardinal date is the often-
quoted mention of the story in the chronicle of
Helinand. This chronicle, as I have shown in
my Epilogue to the 'High History,' cannot
have been written before 1209 nor after 1227,
the probabilities being in favour of the passage
relating to the Graal having been written in
1220. I need not here repeat the evidence on
which this conclusion is based; but I may add
that Guarin, the Bishop of Senlis who con-
trived to lose the last sheets of Helinand's
chronicle, greatly distinguished himself as one
of Philip's ablest generals at the battle of
Bouvines. At that time he was only Bishop-
elect, but he regarded his position as forbidding
him actually to carry arms, and his services

were confined to marshalling the King's forces
and giving orders to the men. The Bishop of
Beauvais on the same occasion renounced the use
of the sword and spear which he had formerly
employed against Richard of England, and
contented himself with a club so as not to
shed the blood of those he might happen to
kill. Both these scrupulously conscientious
prelates will be found, if I am not mistaken, as
the heroes of certain episodes in the 'High
History.'

The notes of time in the manuscripts of the
Graal stories are of very different degrees of
value. One of these occurs in a Prologue
prefixed to several manuscripts of the first part
of the *Conte del Graal*. The Prologue, osten-
sibly written by Crestien de Troyes, announces
that the romance which follows it was 'made
for the most worshipful man that is in the
empire of Rome, to wit, the Count Philip of
Flanders that is worth more than Alexander,
him of whom it is said that he was so very good.'
The pseudo-Crestien then proceeds to contrast
the characters of Philip and Alexander, greatly
to the former's advantage, recording among
other things that 'the gifts which the good
Count Philip bestows are given of charity,'
whereas Alexander 'never cared for charity nor

anything else that is good.' The Philip of
Flanders here referred to has been generally
identified, from the days of Thomas Warton's
History of English Poetry downwards, with
Philip of Alsace, Count of Flanders, who
succeeded his father in 1166, took the Cross in
1188, started for Palestine in 1190, and died of
the plague before Acre in 1191. Warton is
not an authority on whom it is safe to rely
without verification. In this case, however, not
a single one of the many English and foreign
writers who have referred to this Prologue
seems to have taken the trouble to verify
Warton's conclusion. Had they done so, they
would have found that by a very natural mis-
apprehension Warton had mistaken his man.
I have not so much as seen any of the MSS. in
which this Prologue occurs ; but as far as I
can gather from the catalogues of the libraries
in which they are preserved, none of them date
earlier than the fifteenth century. It will have
been observed that the writer dwells repeatedly
and insistently on the 'goodness' of his patron.
If the Prologue was written after 1420,
there can be no reasonable doubt that it was
intended to eulogise, not the Crusader, but the
well-known Philip the Good, Duke of Burgundy, who was born in 1396, became Count

of Flanders in 1419, founded the Order of the Golden Fleece in 1430, and died in 1467. The mere epithet 'good,' as employed by a *trouveur* or chronicler, is, no doubt, insufficient to identify a Count of Flanders. The word, indeed, is applied by Philip Mousquès himself as freely to Philip of Alsace as to any other of the thousand and one notabilities he mentions. In this case, however, the whole and only point in the Prologue is to prove that Philip was 'gooder' than Alexander; and if the Prologue was written after 1420, the inference that the Count Philip of Flanders mentioned is the Philip historically known as 'The Good' is hardly open to question.

Be this as it may, however, the portion of the Prologue referring to Philip and Alexander is obviously an interpolation. The concluding lines which the writer adopts as a tag to his vapid eulogy are part of the original poem, and the misfit of the two portions proclaims at once the interpolator's awkwardness and his suppression of the real prologue. The real prologue, in fact, is nothing else but the Elucidation already translated in full, with the exception of these few lines. They run in English thus :—

'Now will Crestien here recount the ensample that you have heard. Thereof might Crestien well have saved himself the pains, inasmuch as he meaneth to endeavour by the Count's command to set forth in rime the best story that may be told in the King's Court, to wit, the story of the Graal whereof the Count lent him the book. Hearken, therefore, how he delivereth himself.'

As a conclusion to the Elucidation, this is perfectly appropriate and intelligible. The poet says he might well have spared himself the trouble of writing or rehearsing the brief summary or 'ensample' of the story he has already given, because he is about to tell the story itself at length. On the other hand, to tack this passage on to the contrast between Philip and Alexander is simply to reduce it to palpable and irrelevant nonsense. The Prologue-writer is not going to recount the 'ensample' his audience have heard, nor, if he wished to propitiate his patron, could he well have spared his eulogy. A careless scribe may perhaps be responsible for rendering some of his words unintelligible, but the rhymester himself is the culprit guilty of the disastrous discord between his own lines and those of his predecessor.

So far, then, what is certain is that the lines

of the Prologue referring to Philip of Flanders
are an interpolation, and what is probable is
that they are the work of a clumsy story-teller
of the fifteenth century. The elucidator,
indeed, mentions that a count lent him 'the
book,' but this is far indeed from identifying
the lender with Philip of Flanders. It may
be worth while here to quote Warton's own
words : 'Chrestien of Troys wrote *Le Romans
du Graal,* or the adventures of the Sangrale,
which included the deeds of King Arthur, Sir
Tristram, Lancelot du Lake, and the rest of the
knights of the round table before 1191.' When
we inquire where Warton and his followers
discovered this curiously definite point in the
chronology of romantic literature, only one
answer is possible. Warton found, as others
have found, that the Prologue-writer called
himself Crestien, and was effusive in his praises
of Philip of Flanders. He and they thereupon
incontinently identified Crestien with Crestien
de Troies, and Count Philip with the crusader
who went to his reward in 1191. The very
definiteness of the date tells its own story.
There is no more reason to believe that Crestien
wrote the story of the Graal before 1191 than
there is to believe that Crestien was the author
of the Prologue, or that the Philip it refers to

was really the Crusader. When a single tittle of trustworthy evidence is forthcoming that seems to indicate an earlier date than about 1220 for a single line about the Graal written by Crestien de Troies, it will be time enough to consider its value. At present, no such tittle is known to exist.

All difficulty as to the date at which Crestien wrote seems to me removed by the considerations to which I have called attention, but another difficulty in relation to the same writer still remains for after-critics to solve. Long ago, Roquefort denied that any portion of the Romance of the Graal was written by Crestien ; and although the conclusion seems to have been based on insufficient premisses, it still seems probable that much of what is generally attributed to Crestien is really the work of another *trouveur*. The author of *Le Chevalier à l'Épée*, in his introduction to that delightful story, reproaches Crestien for having forgotten to celebrate Messire Gawain among the other warriors of the Table Round. This evidence of a contemporary, and of a kind not open to suspicion, seems to militate strongly against Crestien's authorship of at least those portions of the romance attributed to him in which Messire Gawain is the hero.

The third section of the *Conte del Graal* is the next which gives us more than the name of the writer. With regard to this, there is no occasion to add anything to what Mr. Nutt writes in his valuable *Studies.* 'Manessier has been more explicit ; he describes himself as completing the work at the command of

> Jehanne la Comtesse
> Qu'est de Flandre dame et mestresse.

This Joan, daughter of Baldwin vi., ruled Flanders *alone* during the imprisonment of her husband after the battle of Bouvines (1214-1227), and Manessier's words can only apply to her during this period, so that his continuation must have been written between 1214-1227.'

The next contributor to the story wrote almost at the same time. Robert de Beron, or Bouron, or Borron, informs us that no mortal man had told the story until he had it from

> Mon seigneur Gautier en peis
> Qui de Mont Belyal estoit.

Walter of Montbeliard, who is often in evidence in the history of the Crusades as Constable of Jerusalem and Regent of Cyprus, died in 1212. As Monseigneur's requiem had already been chanted, and he was 'in peace' at the time Robert wrote, it is certain that Robert's contribution cannot have been written before 1212, and probably belongs to several years later.

The claims of Walter Mapes to be regarded as the author of any version or part of any version of the Graal legend may, perhaps, challenge serious discussion when they are seriously put forward. In the thirteenth century to say that a poem was written by Walter Mapes was almost equivalent to saying that the real author was unknown, or wished to remain unknown. The date of Walter's death is uncertain. It is generally assigned to 1210, but this may be three or four years too early.

That Wolfram von Eschenbach won a prize at the minstrel-tournament at Wartburg in 1207, and that he refers in an unfinished poem to the death of Herman Landgrave of Thuringia, which took place in 1216, seem to be the only definite notes of time recoverable with regard to the greatest German poet of the Middle Ages. The date of his *Parzival* is unknown, but that it is later than Crestien's story of the Graal he informs us himself with considerable emphasis. He is said by Rose, I know not on what authority, to have been living in 1227. Mr. Nutt assigns his death to about 1220, but only, I apprehend, on conjectural grounds. Any examination of Wolfram's poems would lead me too far afield, but I may observe that his conception of the Graal as a stone is in strict accordance with other traditions relating to the Holy Vessel. William of Tyre, after describing the siege of Cæsarea in 1102, and the fearful slaughter that took place in the Great Mosque, writes thus : 'In this same Prayer-house was found a vessel of a most clear green colour, shapen after the manner of a dish, which the Genoese aforesaid received by lot instead of a great sum of money, believing it to be made of emerald, and did offer the same to their church as an ornament exceeding precious. Whence it cometh to pass even to this day that whensoever any great folks shall pass through their city, they do of custom display the said vessel as it were a thing marvellous, persuading them that it is in very truth that which the colour thereof doth make show of, to wit, an emerald.' This marvellous vessel is in reality none other than the *Sacro Catino*, or Holy Graal, still preserved in the Cathedral at Genoa. William, it will be observed, makes no mention of its sacred

character. As a matter of fact, its recognition as the Holy Graal did not take place till
many years after William's death, and is first
distinctly recorded in the pages of Jacobus de
Voragine. Wolfram's poem seems to me to
indicate that even in his day the identity of
the stone with the Graal was already an article
of the popular belief. If Wolfram joined the
Albigensian Crusade, which is far from unlikely, it would account for much that remains
unaccounted for in his poem.

The dates I have referred to are, I believe,
all that can with any certainty be relied on
to be found in the various stories of Perceval
and the Graal. They range from about 1210
to about 1230. The Interdict in England
came into force in 1208, and was relaxed in
1214. Every single romance in which the
Curse that fell upon Logres is mentioned was
written either during the Interdict or within
a few years after.

My task is done. I have pointed out what
I believe to be the meaning and motive of the
legends of the Graal, and have shown how
closely some of the cardinal incidents and
personages in the romance are paralleled in the
incidents and personages of contemporary
history. To my own mind, the coincidences

here indicated seem far too many, too coherent, too striking, to be the result of accident. If they are admitted to be the result of deliberate design, even this inadequate introduction may, I hope, be found of some assistance in pioneering the way for future research.

INDEX

N

ABOUT THE AUTHOR

Sebastian Evans was born on 2 March 1830 in Market Bosworth, Leicestershire, the youngest son of Arthur and Anne Dickinson Evans. Evans's father, an Anglican clergyman, master of the local grammar school, and prolific writer of prose and poetry, educated his children himself and communicated his energy and taste for the arts to more than one. John Evans, his brother, became an eminent geologist, archaeologist, and numismatist, served as president of many scientific societies, and was eventually knighted. His sister, Anne Evans, long an invalid, wrote poetry and music; a volume of her works was published posthumously in 1880, with a memoir by Anne Ritchie, Thackeray's daughter.

In 1849 Sebastian Evans won a scholarship to Emmanuel College, Cambridge, where he took his B.A. in 1853. He earned an M.A. in 1857, the year of his marriage to Elizabeth Goldney.

Like many of his Cambridge contemporaries, Evans found his way to the Macmillan's bookshop on Trinity Street. In retrospect, he saw his friendship with Alexander Macmillan as the great educational experience of his undergraduate years, compensation for the stimulation lacking in the normal routines of his college life: "Once in the year we were invited to 'take wine' with the Master, between 'hall' ending at five and 'chapel' beginning at six, and once in every term with the tutor: and these functions afforded our sole opportunities of what was called 'social intercourse' with those dignitaries.... For some of us this sort of go-as-you-please independence was probably wholesome and more stimulating than the stricter restraint of the contemporary system at Oxford, but it left everything to be desired in the way of intellectual training and equipment for the battle of life".

Evans emphasized Macmillan's influence on the religious beliefs of undergraduates, but he was himself never attracted to the theology of F.D. Maurice which Macmillan so eagerly proselytized. He had already developed the idiosyncratic combination of dogmatic scepticism and antipapal bigotry that remained his creed all his life. Macmillan was later to refuse a book of his poems as too aggressively un-Christian; it is a measure of Evans's affection for his publisher that it never appeared under a rival imprint.

Although Evans resented the neglect of his supposed teachers, he knew how to occupy himself profitably. The Macmillan's published his *Sonnets on the Death of the Duke of Wellington* (1852) while he was still an undergraduate, and free copies coaxed complimentary responses from Sir James Stephen and Alfred, Lord Tennyson. Evans also began the study of medieval literature and art that remained a lifelong interest. By the time he left Cambridge to study law at Lincoln's Inn, he had a growing reputation as both poet and artist.

Brother Fabian's Manuscript, and Other Poems, perhaps his best volume of verse, appeared in 1865. Title, subject, and dense blank verse show the extent of Evans's debt to Robert Browning; but, if anything, he is more explicit than his mentor about the corruption of the monastic system. His prioress has had a child by the abbot, and all his clergy connive at producing false miracles, relics, and conversions and live as superstitious, ignorant, cunning parasites on the secular world. The poem shows Evans's verbal facility, sense of the ridiculous, and eccentric learning to advantage.

In 1867 Evans was appointed editor of the Birmingham Daily Gazette. He unsuccessfully contested Birmingham for the Tories in the election of the next year and took his LL.D. from Cambridge. In 1870 he resumed his legal studies. A successful practice on the Oxford circuit did not keep him from journalism, however; in 1878 he founded the *People*, a weekly which he edited for three years.

Evans and his son Frank collaborated on *The Upper Ten*, a translation and adaptation of a French farce, in 1891; it was later republished as *Lady Chillingham's House-Party* (1901). In 1898 he produced his contributions to the study of the Grail legend: a translation of *The High History of the Holy Graal,* which was republished in 1969, and *In Quest of the Holy Graal,* in which he argued that the romance allegorized the events leading up to the Albigensian Crusade. In the same year, his translation of Leo of Assisi's *St. Francis of Assisi,* and *The Mirror of Perfection* appeared. His last major work, a translation of Geoffrey of Monmouth's *twelfth-century history of the kings of Britain,* was published six years later; it was republished with alterations in 1963. Sebastian Evans died on 19 December 1909.